A LOOK AT TODAY'S CHURCHES—
A Comparative Guide

Herbert J. A. Bouman

Publishing House
St. Louis

To Lilly

who has enriched my life and
supported my work in an infinite
variety of Christian concern

Concordia Publishing House, St. Louis Missouri

Preface

This is not a book about religion in general nor about different religions in the world, nor even about the Christian religion as such, though a section is devoted to the basic affirmations of the Christian faith. "A Look at Today's Churches" is not a look at all churches. It deals only with churches and religious groups that are explicitly or implicitly related to Christianity, at least in name. Within the compass of this book there can obviously be no claim to completeness. There are literally hundreds of separate groupings in Christendom, but only a few, chiefly the most prominent in size, duration, impact, controversial status, or aspect of special interest, have been selected for review.

Since these chapters aim at being "a comparative guide" to groups claiming some identification with Christianity, we may well ask what makes a religious body Christian. Is there a universally acceptable and applicable definition or description of the concept "Christian"? What, if any, are the decisive objective criteria by which a church or religious body can be fairly measured as to the degree of its "Christianity"? Surely there is more involved than the name.

The word "Christian" is nearly as old as Christianity itself. Only a short time after Jesus Christ had been raised from the dead and had ascended to heaven, His followers spread out from Jerusalem into other areas of the Mediterranean world. "And in Antioch [Syria] the disciples were for the first time called Christians" (Acts 11:26). Therefore "disciple of Christ" and "Christian" were understood as interchangeable titles. An individual's or a religious body's Christian character is determined by their relation to Christ. The implications of this Biblical teaching should become evident in the body of this book.

The number of churches today is very large. While all Christians stand in relation to Christ, there is wide variety in the understanding of that relationship, a variety that has given rise to endless problems in the history of Christianity. Presenting the differences among churches necessarily leads to making comparisons. Since the author is committed to the "faith, teaching, and confession" of the Lutheran Church, he will naturally write from that perspective. But while he will judge other churches and groups in the light of that commitment, it is his aim to deal with them factually and fairly.

Reformation Day 1979   Herbert J. A. Bouman

Contents

Chapter 1

The Christian Faith

Early in the history of the church, as Christians reflected on their faith and its distinctive character, and as non-Christians were drawn by the power of the Gospel to be united with the church, the Christians assembled the basic elements of the faith in short summaries. These were known as the rule of faith or rule of truth and formed the basis for instructing prospective members and preparing them for Baptism "in the name of the Father and of the Son and of the Holy Spirit." Out of these summaries developed the church's creeds which played a large role in the church's worship. By these creeds, or symbols, Christians recognized one another and professed their difference from all others. They affirmed their belief in one God in opposition to the polytheism of the pagans (1 Corinthians 8:4-6). In distinction from the Jews, who also asserted their monotheism, the Christians expressed their faith in the Holy Trinity, Father, Son, and Holy Spirit: "This is the true Christian faith, that we worship one God in three persons and three persons in one God." There is "one Godhead of the Father and of the Son and of the Holy Spirit, equal in glory and coequal in majesty" (The Athanasian Creed). "We steadfastly maintain that those who believe otherwise do not belong to the church of Christ but are idolaters and blasphemers" (Apology of the Augsburg Confession, I, 2. *The Book of Concord*, Theodore G. Tappert, ed., p. 100). Christians formulated their faith on the basis of the New Testament itself.

The small group of men whom Jesus invited to be associated with Him during His public ministry became ear and eye witnesses of what Jesus said and did. As a result they affirmed Him to be the Christ, the Son of the living God, and they put their faith in Him as their Lord and Savior. Throughout His ministry Jesus promised His disciples the gift of the Holy Spirit, the Spirit of the Father and the Son. On the first Christian Pentecost this promise began to be fulfilled, and the Christian community received remarkable evidences of the Spirit's coming and power. Thus from the beginning Christians verbalized their faith with reference to God the Father, Son, and Holy Spirit. This formed the basic three-part structure of the church's creedal summaries, particularly the Nicene Creed in the East and the Apostles' Creed and the Athanasian Creed in the West.

Though couched in personal terms, "we believe," or "I believe," these crisp statements are mainly an objective recital of Biblical data, revolving around the three Persons of the Holy Trinity and the activity of God as Creator, Redeemer, and Sanctifier. Implicit in these recitals were a number of truths which the Christians considered to be essential elements of their faith.

Christians have always believed that the universe came into being by the creative activity of an almighty and all-wise God and that every person is a creature of God responsible to Him; that humankind rebelled against the Creator and thus brought sin into the world; that by their disobedience human beings have come under God's judgment and have forfeited their fellowship with Him; and that they cannot extricate themselves from their disastrous situation by their own efforts. But Christians also affirm that God the Creator continued to love His fallen creatures and desired to redeem them and restore them to fellowship with Him. God concretely demonstrated His love by sending His eternal Son into this world, into time and history, as a true human being, born of a human mother, given the name Jesus to indicate the purpose of His incarnation: "He shall save His people from their sins." Christians believe that Jesus the Christ fully accomplished God's purpose. By His perfect life and His death on the cross Jesus acted in the stead of all human beings and atoned for their sins. Now God and sinners have been reconciled, and the message goes out to all with the plea to accept God's gift of reconciliation. Christians believe that the Holy Spirit creates in human beings the power to accept God's promise in faith. Christians believe that the restored fellowship with God necessarily leads to a new life-style that manifests itself in a sincere attempt to do God's will and to be of service to fellow human beings.

Christians believe that by their vertical relationship to God through faith all believers at the same time enter a horizontal relationship with all other believers, a fellowship, a community called the church. The church is the body of the exalted Christ, who is the Head, and continues His redemptive activity in the world by proclaiming the Gospel, the recital of God's mighty deeds "for us men and for our salvation," and by administering the Word visibly in the form of the sacraments which the Lord gave His church. Christians believe particularly that Holy Baptism is the entrance-way into the church and that the fellowship manifests itself concretely and intimately in the Holy Communion, the fellowship meal. Christians believe that the fellowship is there for mutual assistance, admonition, and encouragement, from which no believer should isolate himself. The weal or woe of one member affects all other members.

Christians believe that existence on this earth is not the end but that there will be a resurrection of all the dead at the end of time and that God's gift is eternal life through faith in Jesus Christ.

This, in spite of all individual differences in understanding and interpretation, represents the basic summary of the meaning of "Christian" and what, in the words of a fifth-century theologian, Vincent of Lerins, "was always, everywhere, and by all believed" and was assembled in the "ecumenical," or "catholic," creeds. It was felt that any major deviation from this statement of the faith created serious tensions and called into question the Christianity of those who deviated. The ecumenical creeds gave the answer to the twofold question: "What do all Christians have in common, and how are they distinguished from adherents of other religions, such as Judaism, Islam, Hinduism, and Buddhism?"

Prominent in the Christian concern was the sense of solidarity on the part of all believers, though separated by long distances, language, culture, etc. Christians remembered the Lord's promise: "I will build my church," in the singular, not "churches." They recalled the apostle's great stress on oneness: ". . . eager to maintain the unity of the Spirit in the bond of peace. There is one body and one Spirit, just as you were called to the one hope that belongs to your call, one Lord, one faith, one baptism, one God and Father of us all, who is above all and through all and in all" (Ephesians 4:3-6). This is reflected in the church's belief about the church as "one, holy, catholic (or Christian), apostolic." Christians were mindful of the Lord's prayer concerning those who believe in Him through the ministry of the apostolic word "that they may all be one" (John 17:21).

What has been sketched here represents the design of the church's Founder and Lord. The New Testament, especially in the letters of the apostles, teems with admonitions to Christians to avoid all that would jeopardize their unity and to be diligent about all that would serve to preserve and strengthen it. That is the ideal that has never been realized in the history of the church and certainly is not so today.

Christendom is divided into literally hundreds of church groups maintaining separate names and separate existence. A popular Christian hymn speaks of the church as "by schisms rent asunder, by heresies distressed." People have spoken of "our unity in Christ and the scandal of our disunity as churches." There have not always been as many divisions as there are now, but the spirit of factionalism has manifested itself throughout the church's history, even in the days of the apostles. St. Paul attacks this spirit in the church at Corinth: "I appeal to you, brethren, by the name of our Lord Jesus Christ, that all of you agree and that there be no dissensions among you. . . . each one of you says, 'I belong to Paul,' or 'I belong to Apollos,' or 'I belong to Cephas.' or 'I belong to Christ.' Is Christ divided?" (1 Corinthians 1:10-13). Among the works of the flesh are listed strife, dissension, and party spirit (Galatians 5:20). In the early church there soon developed groups which separated from the main church because of divergent interpretations or emphases with regard to the Christian message.

A major split in the church occurred in the eleventh century when a rift came between the Eastern, or Greek, Christians and the Western, or Latin, Christians, a rift that has continued to the present day. Also in Western Christendom there were at various times smaller or larger groups that disagreed with what the church taught or practiced, and they separated from the church. Even when there was no outward separation, there were philosophical and theological systems within the church in vigorous opposition to each other. Thus the church was not really one already in the centuries before the Reformation.

The sixteenth century produced major divisions in Western Christendom. Martin Luther in Saxony, Ulrich Zwingli in Zurich (German Switzerland), and John Calvin in Geneva (French Switzerland) were the principal protagonists of major reform movements in the faith and life of the church. In addition, there were externally more radical currents in opposition to the church of Rome, such as the Anabaptists and Mennonites. In England the reform movement followed its own course. To promote the unity of her kingdom, Queen Elizabeth I helped bring about the so-called "Elizabethan Settlement" of the religious question in the Thirty-nine Articles of the Church of England and in the Book of Common Prayer. These documents pursued a "comprehensive policy" in that large elements of pre-Reformation Anglican Catholicism were merged with considerable amounts of theology from Lutheran and Calvinist sources. In Europe, therefore, down to modern times, many books on the religious bodies included treatment of four or five separate churches: Orthodox, Roman Catholic, Lutheran, Reformed, and Anglican. Until recently the ties between church and state in many European countries were quite close, as they had been ever since the days of Constantine I (ca. 280—337 A.D.), the first Christian emperor of the Roman Empire.

The new situation is markedly different in the United States of America, "the new world." The great watchword in the birth of this nation was freedom: freedom from oppressive government, freedom from state control of religion, freedom of speech, press, religion, peaceable assembly, enunciated in a Bill of Rights which guarantees the rights and liberties of the individual person. "Congress shall make no law respecting the establishment of religion." This has had a far-reaching effect on the existence and life of the church in America. Citizenship with its attendant rights and privileges of franchise, property, public office, etc. was not linked to church membership. While the government looked with favor upon the practice of religion as a significant aid in public morale and morals, in the "maintenance of righteousness and the hindrance and punishment of wickedness," and therefore granted religious bodies protection and exemption from corporate taxes, the government did not favor one church above another and provided no subsidies. In the spirit of religious voluntarism the American was free to choose church membership or reject it and affiliate with the body of his choice or none at all, without incurring civil pressures or disabilities. It was up to the people themselves to raise the money for their church's programs.

The results were quite predictable: On the one hand, since the people were members of the church because they wanted to be and not because they had to be, there was very much personal interest in and support of the church and a high rate of regular attendance at the church's worship services, much better than in European state churches. On the other hand, the absence of civil constraints caused multitudes to become or remain completely unchurched and have no living connection with the church whatever. Furthermore, the government's scrupulous hands-off policy and its leaning over backward so that there be no mingling of church and state has undoubtedly contributed profoundly to the increasing secularization of American culture.

Yet another consequence of the American system has been a staggering proliferation and multiplication of churches, church groups, and cultic and sectarian movements. Where European writers generally dealt with four or five churches, the observer of the religious scene in America is confronted by hundreds of corporate entities, each with its own name and its distinctive characteristics or teachings. It is no wonder that the American church scene is often completely bewildering to outsiders and even to Americans themselves. No wonder thoughtful people bewail the "scandal of our disunity as churches." No wonder the earnest seeker is confused as he sees the scores of varieties of churches dotting the landscape and competing with each other for the uncommitted citizen, or even attempting to lure members of other churches, and each with its own distinctive truth claims.

Many are not only confused by the situation but deeply offended. How, they ask, can the enmity and rivalry among churches, all claiming to speak for Jesus Christ, reflect anything but disgrace upon Christianity as a whole? No wonder many of the churches are experiencing widespread apostasy among their members. It is quite in agreement with the facts presented by the spirit of our time to say that the church as a whole has become irrelevant to a majority of Americans. The line of demarcation between the church and secular society has been largely obliterated. It is in a setting such as this that present-day Christians are called upon to reflect anew on their faith and seek to understand its implications for their relationship to other Christians and their fellow human beings in general.

Chapter 2

Ancient Traditions

A. The Orthodox Church

The oldest continuous Christian church is the Holy Oriental Catholic and Apostolic Church, sometimes known as the Greek Orthodox, Eastern Orthodox, or simply the Orthodox Church, which claims between three and four million members in the United States. Its roots are in Palestine, and its greatest flowering and sphere of influence in the countries of the Eastern Mediterranean, including North Africa, Asia Minor, Greece, the Balkans, and the Slavic lands of Eastern Europe, especially Russia. There are a number of independent churches, mostly along ethnic and national lines, but all are in fellowship with the patriarch of Constantinople, who is titled Ecumenical Patriarch.

Orthodox faith is characterized by antiquity, conservatism, traditionalism, simplicity, mysticism, and highly developed liturgical worship. Emphasis on its antiquity has sometimes led almost to an identification of the old with the orthodox and often to strong opposition to the introduction of anything new or different in practice. Orthodox reverence for the old finds expression in the church's conservatism.

There was good reason for this conservatism. During most of the church's history it had to exist under political domination. Constantine, the first Christian Roman emperor, moved the imperial capital to Byzantium and renamed it Constantinople, the modern Istanbul. From then on the Eastern part of the church was largely controlled by the successors of Constantine. The seventh century saw the rise of Islam, whose missionary zeal spread the Mohammedan religion throughout the territory of Orthodoxy and assumed a dominant role. Although the Christians were not exterminated, they were discriminated against in a variety of ways that limited their civil liberties and reduced them to the status of second-class citizens. In more modern times the largest constituency by far was the Russian church. In the days of Peter the Great in the seventeenth century, the church was placed under direct Czarist control. In our own time the church in Russia is largely subject to the Communist regime.

Thus through much of its history the Orthodox church has existed under varying kinds and degrees of oppression and suppression. It was often a question of bare survival for Christians in those areas. In consequence, the Christians tended to cling tenaciously to the elements of the faith they had received, to conserve the essentials of their religion at all costs. There was little opportunity or inclination to reflect on the faith or think through the relationship of the individual items of the Biblical witness to each other or their implications for faith and life.

Another important factor in the life of Eastern Orthodoxy was its considerable isolation from the rest of the Christian world. Language and cultural and political barriers in themselves made communication difficult enough. But the great schism of 1054 erected walls of separation that have not been completely breached to the present day. When the Moslem Turks gained control over most of the territory of Orthodoxy, the isolation became even more comprehensive. As a result Eastern Christianity had almost no contact with the further development of Christian thought in the West and did not share in the ferment of new ideas.

The Eastern church was, therefore, affected in a very limited way by the mighty theological and ecclesiological currents that so profoundly influenced Western Europe, such as centuries of scholasticism, Christian humanism, and the 16th-century Reformation. Consequently, in comparison with the West, Eastern Christianity is characterized by a simple, elementary, largely unreflected theology. The faith has been formulated and is enshrined in the Nicene Creed and the doctrinal decisions of the first seven ecumenical councils, all in the East, in which Eastern churchmen participated, 325 to 787. Great emphasis is placed on the Divine Liturgy, the elaborate and often splendid worship services where the faith is, in a sense, reenacted and experienced in a mystical way rather than discussed intellectually.

On the other hand, since Eastern and Western Christians were, after all, united for a thousand years before the split, a considerable consensus in doctrine and practice might be expected. This is indeed the case. Eastern Orthodoxy has many of the same beliefs and practices as Roman Catholicism, except that there is much less scholastic detail and much less official dogmatic fixation and far less development.

For the Orthodox all teaching is drawn from Holy Tradition, either as recorded in the Scriptures or as handed down orally from

Christ and the apostles. In the doctrine of the Holy Trinity, the emphasis is on the Father as the Source of all, including the other Persons of the Godhead. The Son is born of the Father, and the Holy Spirit proceeds from the Father. Therefore the Eastern version of the Nicene Creed omits from the third article the words "and the Son" *(Filioque)* with reference to the Holy Spirit's proceeding.

Western Christian theology has attempted to illustrate its understanding of the doctrine of the Holy Trinity by means of an equilateral triangle or three interlocking circles. Christians in the Western tradition believe it to be Biblical teaching that Father, Son, and Holy Spirit share fully in one another's properties. In the Third Article of the Nicene Creed as used in Western churches it is stated that "the Holy Spirit proceeds from the Father *and the Son,*" not just "from the Father," as in the Orthodox Church.

All people are creatures of God and are sinners. However, the fall into sin is regarded more as a being deprived than a being depraved; serious but not fatal. There is, therefore, a more optimistic view of man's natural potential. In the Eastern view of God there is heavy emphasis on God's essential goodness. Salvation is indeed achieved by the incarnation and sacrifice and, above all, the resurrection of Jesus Christ. The sinner receives salvation through his faith as supplemented by his deeds.

Like Roman Catholics, the Orthodox have seven sacraments, or "mysteries." Holy Baptism is administered to infants by triple immersion, followed immediately by Chrismation (Confirmation), anointing with holy oil for the impartation of the Holy Spirit. In the Eucharist the bread and wine become the body and blood of Christ by action of the Holy Spirit who is invoked upon the elements in a special prayer called *Epiklesis.* Both elements are distributed to the communicants by intinction, a morsel of bread in a spoonful of wine. The clergy may be married before receiving Holy Orders, but not afterwards. Bishops are chosen from among celibate monks. Marriage and Penance and Holy Unction are the other sacraments. The last named is applied not so much to prepare for death as to aid in the person's recovery.

In distinction from Western Catholics the Orthodox do not accept the claims of supreme authority and infallibility made for the pope; they accord him the honor of being one of five peers, together with the patriarchs of Jerusalem, Antioch, Alexandria, and Constantinople. The Virgin Mary is honored as Mother of God, but there is no dogma of her immaculate conception or bodily assumption. By contrast, since 1854 it is an official teaching of the Roman Catholic Church that "the most Blessed Virgin Mary in the first instant of her conception ... was preserved free from all stain of original sin. . . ." Since 1950 it is likewise an official teaching of the Roman Catholic Church that "the Immaculate Mother of God, Mary ever Virgin, after her life on earth, was assumed, body and soul, to the glory of heaven." In the Eastern church the saints are revered through holy icons, or painted pictures, but there is no mention of the merits of the saints. The Orthodox do not teach the existence of a purgatory, a place where, according to Roman Catholic teaching souls are purged or cleansed before entering heaven. But they believe there continues to be some kind of inter-communication between the departed and the living; they are said to pray for each other. In recent years Orthodox churches have moved out of their isolation and have participated extensively in ecumenical affairs such as the World Council of Churches and dialog with several other church bodies.

B. The Roman Catholic Church

By far the largest Christian body is the Roman Catholic Church, so called because its headquarters are in Rome and the language of its official pronouncements and, until recently, its liturgy has for many centuries been the language of Rome, Latin. Worldwide Catholicism is so large and complex that it is difficult to capture its infinite variety in a few paragraphs. It used to be said that "Rome is always the same" *(Roma semper eadem)*, but that is true only with considerable qualification. We may speak of at least three different "Romes": Western Catholicism in the late Middle Ages, the post-Reformation Roman church (Council of Trent, 1545-1563, to mid-twentieth century), and the church since the Second Vatican Council. Frank S. Mead states:

In view of the amazing reforms and changes which have swept the Roman Catholic Church since Pope John XXIII, it has become almost impossible to emphasize any detail in doctrine; a new era of open discussion and broad interpretation is prevalent in the whole church, and changes come swiftly *(Handbook of Denominations in the United States*, 5th ed. Nashville: Abingdon Press, 1970, p. 192).

Rome has indeed changed. However, it is a change in accent and in practice rather than in basic teaching. "Doctrine remains, however, deeply rooted in the rock of the 4 historic creeds" (Mead, ibid.) The four creeds are the three ancient ecumenical symbols, Apostles', Nicene, and Athanasian, plus the Creed of Pius IV from the Council of Trent. Western Christendom can look back on many brilliant theological thinkers: Tertullian, Augustine, Thomas Aquinas, Peter Lombard, Bonaventure, Anselm of Canterbury, and scores of others whose writings have greatly influenced Western theology and contributed to its well-nigh infinite detail.

Yet there are several elements in Roman Catholicism that have traditionally set it apart from other churches. Among these elements are the church's polity or government, the sacramental system, purgatory, and the place of the Virgin Mary and the saints in the faith and life of members.

While there are other churches with a hierarchical form of church government (several ranks of clergy, such as bishop, priest, deacon) and the claim of an ordained clergy reaching back in an unbroken line to the apostles, the church of Rome has a unique chain of authority headed by the pope. In all matters pertaining to faith, morals, and discipline his authority is supreme, even above that of a council of the whole church. When the pope speaks in his official capacity as "Vicar of Christ on earth and the Visible Head of the Church" *(ex cathedra)* with the intention of teaching the church, he speaks infallibly. Although the accents have shifted since Vatican II and some degree of power is granted to regional synods of bishops, there is ultimately no authority apart from the pope and certainly not in opposition to the pope.

Obviously no one person can administer so vast and complex a body as the Roman church. The pope is assisted by a large number of standing boards or commissions, called congregations, plus tribunals and secretariats. Together they constitute the Roman Curia. These structures are designed to deal with a great variety of issues, such as the church's official dogmas, the sacraments, liturgical matters, education, missions, the clergy, relations to Oriental churches, and cases of discipline. A more recent addition and an outgrowth of Vatican II are the secretariats for the promotion of Christian unity, for non-Christians, and for nonbelievers.

There is a very close connection between the ordained clergy and the total life of the members. The priest receives his authority and power for a valid ministry through the Sacrament of Holy Orders. This enables him to administer the other six sacraments validly and thus aid the faith and life of the parishioners at various ages and under various circumstances with the application of an appropriate sacrament.

The Christian, at almost every important state of his mortal career, finds at his side the priest with power received from God, in the act of communicating or increasing that grace which is the supernatural life of his soul.

Scarcely is he born before the priest, baptizing him, brings him a new birth to a more noble and precious life, a supernatural life, and makes him a son of God and of the Church of Jesus Christ.

To strengthen him to fight bravely in spiritual combats, a priest invested with special dignity [a bishop] makes him a soldier of Christ by holy Chrism [confirmation].

Then, as soon as he is able to recognize and value the Bread of Angels [the Eucharist], the priest gives It to him, the living and life-giving Food come down from heaven.

If he falls, the priest raises him up again in the name of God, and reconciles him to God with the Sacrament of Penance.

Again, if he is called by God to found a family and to collaborate with Him in the transmission of human life throughout the world, thus increasing the number of the faithful on earth, and thereafter the ranks of the elect in Heaven, the priest is there to bless his espousals and unblemished love; and when finally, arrived at the portals of eternity, the Christian feels the need of strength and courage before presenting himself at the tribunal of the Divine Judge, the priest with the holy Oils anoints the failing members of the sick or dying Christian, and reconsecrates and comforts him.

Thus the priest accompanies the Christian throughout the pilgrimage of this life to the gates of Heaven. He accompanies the body to its restingplace in the grave with rites and prayers of immortal life. And even beyond the threshold of eternity he follows the soul to aid it with Christian suffrages, if need there be of further purification [purgatory] and alleviation. Thus, from the cradle to the grave the priest is ever beside the faithful, a guide, a solace, a minister of salvation and dispenser of grace and blessing (Encyclical of Pius XI, *Ad Catholici Sacerdotii*, December 1935, cited in Stanley I. Stuber, *Primer on Roman Catholicism for Protestants*. New York: Association Press, 1953, pp. 75 f.).

Salvation is by the grace of God, this grace having been provided by the merits of Christ, plus the merits of the Virgin Mary and the saints. Grace is thought of in quantitative terms, as spiritual strength, as a supernatural gift, which is conveyed through the sacraments as the means of grace and infused into hearts, thus enabling people to do good works and earn merit.

Through Holy Baptism one is taken into church membership and may receive the rest of the sacraments. Baptism is absolutely necessary for full salvation. Unbaptized infants are therefore consigned to a place called limbo *(limbus infantum)*, where they may have a degree of natural happiness but where they are forever excluded from the beatific vision of God in paradise.

If a child dies without Baptism, the soul is sent into eternity with the stain of original sin upon it. In such a state it can never see the Face of that God who created it, nor can it ever enter the Kingdom of Heaven for which it was destined (From *A Manual for Nurses*, cited in Stuber, p. 157).

Since Baptism is absolutely indispensable, anyone may baptize in an emergency. Also, there are substitutes for water Baptism if it is unattainable, the so-called Baptism of Desire, an intense love and longing for God, and the Baptism of Blood, undergoing martyrdom for Jesus' sake.

Through their Baptism all people are said to become members of the Roman Catholic Church and therefore subject to its government and laws. "Every baptised person is subject to the jurisdiction of the Church" (Ludwig Ott, *Fundamentals of Catholic Dogma*, ed. in English by James Bastible. St. Louis: B. Herder Book Co., 1958, p. 336. See also p. 311: "Thus the Church claims jurisdiction over baptised persons who are separated from her").

Confirmation must be administered by a bishop, and it imparts the gift of the Holy Spirit. The Sacrament of Penance provides for the confession and forgiveness of sins committed after Baptism. Members are required to make confession at least once a year.

The celebration of the Mass is the focus of Roman Catholic liturgy and worship. It has even influenced the architecture of churches, so that the worshiper's eye is drawn directly to the high altar, on which reposes the consecrated host, the eucharistic presence of Christ. The Mass consists of several distinct parts. One is the act of taking the host, or wafer, which the priest has transubstantiated into Christ's very body by speaking the words of institution, and offering it as a sacrifice to God for the sins of living and dead. Another part is the distribution of the consecrated hosts to the communicants. The general practice is to withhold the wine from the communicants, although, since Vatican II, "communion under both kinds may be granted when the bishops think fit, not only to clerics and religious, but also to the laity." (*Constitution on the Sacred Liturgy*, par. 55, in: *The Documents of Vatican II*, Walter M. Abbott, ed. New York: Guild Press, 1966, p. 156). In addition, the host is elevated for reverence by the worshipers. On Thursday after Trinity Sunday the host is carried through the streets (especially in Roman Catholic countries) in observance of the *Corpus Christi* festival. All communicants are commanded to receive the Eucharist during the Easter season.

The Sacrament of Holy Orders, performed by a bishop, places the candidate into the apostolic succession of priests and endows him with special powers and graces for his office. A distinction is made between the so-called "secular" parish priests and the "religious," or members of monastic orders. For all of them the ban against marriage still stands, although the clergy of the so-called Uniate churches may be married once. These are priests of Eastern churches following the customs and practices of the Orthodox Church but accepting the pope as head of the church.

Marriage is considered sacramental when performed by a priest. Roman Catholics are generally forbidden to be divorced on pain of excommunication, but there may be annulments, implying that the marriage was not valid to begin with. Marriage with members of other churches is strongly discouraged. But if a Catholic does marry a non-Catholic, the marriage is to be performed by a priest and the non-Catholic must agree: (1) not to interfere with the Catholic's exercise of his or her religion; (2) to have all children baptized and reared in the Catholic Church. However, many such marriages are now being celebrated with Protestant clergy participation, and the two agreements are not always fulfilled.

Extreme Unction is designed to prepare the dying person for a blessed death. It may be administered even when there appear to be no more vital signs.

The Second Vatican Council (October 11, 1962—December 8, 1965) offers an up-to-date authoritative summary of the sacramental system:

It is through the sacraments and the exercise of the virtues that the sacred nature and organic structure of the priestly community is brought into operation. Incorporated into the Church

19

through baptism, the faithful are consecrated by the baptismal character to the exercise of the cult of the Christian religion. Reborn as sons of God, they must confess before men the faith which they have received from God through the Church. Bound more intimately to the Church by the Sacrament of Confirmation, they are endowed by the Holy Spirit with special strength. Hence they are more strictly obliged to spread and defend the faith both by word and by deed as true witnesses of Christ.

Taking part in the Eucharistic Sacrifice, which is the fount and apex of the whole Christian life, they offer the divine Victim to God, and offer themselves along with it. Thus, both by the act of oblation and through holy Communion, all perform their proper part in this liturgical service, not, indeed, all in the same way but each in that way which is appropriate to himself. Strengthened anew at the holy table by the Body of Christ, they manifest in a practical way that unity of God's People which is suitably signified and wondrously brought about by this most awesome sacrament.

Those who approach the Sacrament of Penance obtain pardon from the mercy of God for offenses committed against Him. They are at the same time reconciled with the Church, which they have wounded by their sins, and which by charity, example, and prayer seeks their conversion. By the sacred anointing of the sick and the prayer of her priests, the whole Church commends those who are ill to the suffering and glorified Lord, asking that He may lighten their suffering and save them (cf. James 5:14-16). She exhorts them, moreover, to contribute to the welfare of the whole People of God by associating themselves freely with the passion and death of Christ (cf. Romans 8:17; Colossians 1:24; 2 Timothy 2:11-12; 1 Peter 4:13). Those of the faithful who are consecrated by holy orders are appointed to feed the Church in Christ's name with the Word and the grace of God.

Finally, Christian spouses, in virtue of the sacrament of matrimony, signify and partake of the mystery of that unity and fruitful love which exists between Christ and His Church (cf. Ephesians 5:32). The spouses thereby help each other to attain to holiness in their married life and by the rearing and education of their children. And so, in their state and way of life, they have their own special gift among the People of God (cf. 1 Corinthians 7:7).

. . . .

Fortified by so many and such powerful means of salvation, all the faithful, whatever their condition or state, are called by the Lord, each in his own way, to that perfect holiness whereby the Father Himself is perfect (The Dogmatic Constitution of the Church, par. 11, in: *The Documents of Vatican II*, pp. 27 ff.).

Vatican II was the outgrowth of Pope John XXIII's wish to "open the windows and let in some fresh air." The mood was one of *Aggiornamento*, of renewal and updating. After John's death, Pope Paul VI continued the Council until its conclusion. Official observers were invited from the major non-Catholic churches. While there was no change in the church's official teaching (dogma), there were significant restatements, clarifications, and emendations of traditional formulations. There was a genuine attempt to be considerate of non-Catholic sensitivities and to open the way for inter-Christian dialog. There was also a thorough revision of liturgical forms and practices, so that the Mass may be celebrated in the vernacular, communicants may be given both wafer and wine, more emphasis is placed on preaching, etc. Between 40 and 50 million Americans are affiliated with the Roman Catholic church.

Chapter 3

Early Reformation

A. The Lutheran Church

The Lutheran Church is one of a very small number of churches whose names perpetuate names of men. The name Lutheran was not self-chosen but applied from without as a term of derision. When Martin Luther first heard of this, he was appalled:

> In the first place, I ask that men make no reference to my name; let them call themselves Christians, not Lutherans. What is Luther? After all, the teaching is not mine. Neither was I crucified for anyone (*Luther's Works*, American Edition, Vol. 45, p. 70).

Only a few months later, when he felt that the identification was understood to mean acknowledgment of the truth of his teaching, he counseled:

> But if you are convinced that Luther's teaching is in accord with the Gospel and that the pope's is not, then you should not discard Luther so completely, lest with him you discard also his teaching, which you nevertheless recognize as Christ's teaching (*Luther's Works*, Vol. 36, p. 265).

As a matter of fact, whenever the "Reformation" is mentioned, the person who most readily comes to mind and is most generally associated with the Reformation is Luther. He is one of a small number of people who have profoundly influenced the course of history. Much has been written about the nationalistic, literary, and sociological aspects of his career in 16th-century Germany. What concerns us here particularly is his impact on the theology and life of the church.

Luther was a devout son of the Roman Church. He was characterized by an extremely sensitive conscience. Uppermost in his mind was the question: "How may I get a gracious God?" His conscience filled him with a deep consciousness of guilt and relentlessly drove him to seek deliverance from his sins. Medieval piety viewed God as a God of justice who rewarded good deeds and punished bad ones. God was also seen as the source of grace in the sense of imparting to man quantities of spiritual strength, thus enabling man to do good works and cooperate with God in achieving salvation and God's favor. Luther conscientiously pursued this course, but no matter how hard he tried to live up to what he conceived God's justice to be and what was demanded of him, he found no peace. He was driven to despair. It was only the advice to look away from himself, his own sin and guilt, and look to "the wounds of Christ" that rescued him and appeased his quest for a gracious God.

This discovery, or rediscovery, of the Gospel revolutionized Luther's whole life, his theology, his ethics, his interpretation of the Scriptures, as well as his understanding of the church. Now he saw God not only as the God of justice who demanded perfection, but above all as the God of mercy and love who through Jesus Christ bestowed forgiveness and righteousness as free gifts; the majestic Creator of the universe was adored as the loving Father. Near the end of his life Luther reminisced about this decisive breakthrough in his career, recalling especially his difficulty in understanding St. Paul's phrase in Romans 1:17, the "righteousness of God." After much wrestling with the concept, the meaning of the passage finally dawned on him:

At last, by the mercy of God, meditating day and night, I gave heed to the context of the words, namely, "In it the righteousness of God is revealed, as it is written, 'He who through faith is righteous shall live.'" There I began to understand that the righteousness of God is that by which the righteous lives by a gift of God, namely by faith. And this is the meaning: the righteousness of God is revealed by the Gospel, namely, the passive righteousness with which merciful God justifies us by faith, as it is written, "He who through faith is righteous shall live." Here I felt that I was altogether born again and had entered paradise itself through open gates. There a totally other face of the entire Scripture showed itself to me (*Luther's Works*, Vol. 34, p. 337).

Because of the emphasis on the primacy of the Gospel, the movement inaugurated by Luther came to be called "evangelical," proclaiming the Gospel and teaching theology from the perspective of the Gospel. It was inevitable that Luther, having come to this conviction, would subsequently review and judge all aspects of the church's teaching and practice from this perspective. And since Luther had been led to his assurance through an understanding of St. Paul's letter to the Romans, the language and thought of St. Paul tended to dominate Luther's theological expression. Justification by grace alone, received by faith alone, became central to his formulations.

Luther's position at the University of Wittenberg enabled him to share his findings with his colleagues and students. Through his many theological works, often written in popular style, Luther exerted an influence throughout Europe, far beyond his native Saxony. Thus what began as one man's quest for a gracious God had developed into a powerful religious movement for renewal and reform. In 1530 Luther's supporters offered the emperor and Diet of the German nation at Augsburg their statement of faith, called the Augsburg Confession. During the next fifty years this document was supplemented and further clarified by a number of additional documents, but it remained the primary affirmation of the Lutheran position, and the churches that adopted it called themselves churches of the Augsburg Confession. They said, "We consider this Confession a genuinely Christian symbol which all true Christians ought to accept next to the Word of God, just as in ancient times Christian symbols and confessions were formulated in the church of God." (Tappert, *Book of Concord*, p. 502). "And we do not intend, either in this or in subsequent doctrinal statements, to depart from the aforementioned Confession or to set up a different and new confession" (ibid.). "This symbol distinguishes our reformed [Lutheran] churches from the papacy and from other condemned sects and heresies" (ibid., p. 504).

The Lutheran movement has been called the "conservative reformation." Indeed, the conservation of the church's heritage reaching back to the early centuries is characteristic of Lutheranism. Lutherans are explicit in their commitment to the creeds of the ancient church, "accepted as the unanimous, catholic, Christian faith and confessions of the orthodox and true church" (Tappert, p. 465). They accepted the arrangement of the church year and most of the traditional forms of worship. They were also willing to continue traditional forms of church government. Here, too, the Gospel provided the criterion. Traditions that were believed to promote the welfare and good order of the church and thus aid the proclamation of the Gospel were taken over unchanged; traditions that as such were useful but had been overlaid with accretions regarded as injurious to the Gospel were adopted in a purified form; traditions which in themselves appeared to the Lutherans to be inimical to the Gospel were eliminated. Ancient and medieval elements of catechetical instruction were retained and augmented. The sacraments were interpreted as added forms of the Gospel. Luther wrote regarding the Gospel that it

> offers counsel and help against sin in more than one way, for God is surpassingly rich in his grace: First, through the spoken word, by which the forgiveness of sin (the peculiar office of the Gospel) is preached to the whole world; second, through Baptism; third, through the holy Sacrament of the Altar; fourth, through the power of keys [absolution]; and finally, through the mutual conversation and consolation of brethren (Smalcald Articles, Part III, Article IV; Tappert, p. 310).

The Gospel perspective also controls the Lutheran approach to the Sacred Scriptures. While they are indeed the inspired Word of God and express God's will for mankind, including His legal demands and judgments, the Scriptures center in Jesus Christ, the Word made flesh, the revelation of God's mercy. This Gospel message is not only the Bible's principal content but also the basic principle of interpretation. In connection with the justifying Gospel it is said that it is

> of especial service for the clear, correct understanding of the entire Holy Scriptures, and alone shows the way to the unspeakable treasure and right knowledge of Christ, and alone opens the door to the entire Bible (Apology of the Augsburg Confession, Article IV, according to the German version, cited in *Triglot Concordia*, St. Louis: Concordia Publishing House, 1921, p. 121).

Unlike others in the 16th century, the Lutherans showed no particular interest in defining the limits of the list of books that belong into the Bible beyond speaking of the "prophetic and apostolic writings of the Old and New Testaments." Their concern lay in being confronted in the Scriptures by the God of mercy in Jesus Christ, through whom men were delivered from the God of judgment.

Lutherans describe the church as the "assembly of all believers among whom the Gospel is preached in its purity and the holy sacraments are administered according to the Gospel" (Augsburg Confession, VII, Tappert, p. 32). External organization and form of church government are not essential parts of the definition. With regard to the ministry the emphasis is not on an institution that stands in apostolic succession but on a function, to insure the preaching of the Gospel and the administration of the sacraments. Since a local assembly or congregation of believers gathers around the preached Gospel and the administered sacraments, the means through which the Holy Spirit causes Christ to be present, the congregation has all the authority that exists in the church as a whole.

For Lutherans Christian ethics are entirely the outgrowth of faith in Christ. The Christian's good works are, therefore, the result of being justified by faith; they contribute nothing of merit to the Christian's relation to God. "When through faith the Holy Spirit is given, the heart is moved to do good works" (Augsburg Confession, XX, 29. Tappert, p. 45).

Lutherans throughout the world constitute the largest of the churches that have come out of the 16th-century Reformation, numbering some 70,000,000 members, of whom between 9 and 10 million live in the United States and Canada. Approximately 50 million are associated with the Lutheran World Federation. The great majority of church members in northern Europe, in Denmark, Norway, Sweden, Finland, and northern Germany, are affiliated with the Lutheran Church.

B. The Protestant Episcopal Church (The Anglican Communion)

The name "Protestant Episcopal" declares that it is non-Roman and that it believes in a polity, or church government, by a graded hierarchy of the clergy (bishops, priests, and deacons). While completely independent, the Protestant Episcopal Church is the American branch of the Anglican Communion, a worldwide fellowship associated with the Church of England. In doctrine, discipline, and worship there is essential agreement.

The isolation of the British Isles contributed to a degree of independence from Roman control higher than that of continental European churches. Political history greatly influenced the development of this church's doctrine and practice. King Henry VIII forced separation from the pope's government so that the king could be supreme in England in both state and church. On Henry's part there was little inclination to change any of the doctrines of the Roman Church. At the same time, the writings of the Lutheran Reformation in Germany and, somewhat later, of the Calvinist Reformation in Switzerland found their way into England and had a powerful impact on religious faith and thought among the people. Under Henry's son,

Edward VI, *The Book of Common Prayer* and the 42 Articles of Religion were written. When Elizabeth I ascended the throne, she decided that it would be in her country's best interests to be aligned with the Protestant lands of Europe. Aware of the Roman Catholic, Lutheran, and Calvinist crosscurrents, the queen called for a statement of faith that might be acceptable to all or at least the majority of her subjects. This led to the formulation of the 39 articles, the noted Elizabethan Settlement, which pursued a "comprehensive policy." The Church of England desired to be "Catholic, but not Roman, Protestant but neither Lutheran nor Calvinist," although all of these diverse elements continued strong in England.

It is an interesting little historical sidelight that one of the titles of the British sovereign is "Defender of the Faith." It was awarded to Henry VIII by the pope in appreciation of that monarch's attack on Martin Luther. This title remains one of the royal designations to the present day, although the British sovereign is now the "Defender" of a somewhat different "Faith."

Ultimately there developed several distinct forms of Anglican faith and worship, known popularly as "high church," "low church," and "broad church." "High church," also know as Anglo-Catholicism, aims at perpetuating or restoring early, pre-Roman Catholicism with strong emphasis on liturgical and sacramental worship. "Low church," also called Evangelical, refers to less formal worship, more stress on preaching, and Protestant (especially Calvinist) doctrine. "Broad church" designates the movement which minimizes doctrinal differences and emphasizes an intellectual approach and generally identifies with theological liberalism.

Claiming to be both Catholic and Protestant, it [the Anglican Church] combines the ritual and polity of Catholicism with a moderately Calvinistic theology. Episcopalians assert that they resist the "additions of Romanism and the subtractions of Protestantism" (William J. Whalen, *Separated Brethren*. Milwaukee: The Bruce Publishing Co., 1961, p. 61).

Since 1888 the churches of the Anglican Communion regard the so-called Lambeth Quadrilateral as a sufficient platform for Christian unity:

a) The Holy Scriptures of the Old and New Testaments as "containing all things necessary to salvation," and as being the rule and ultimate standard of faith.

27

b) The Apostles' Creed as the baptismal symbol, and the Nicene Creed as the sufficient statement of the Christian faith.

c) The two sacraments ordained by Christ Himself— Baptism and the Supper of the Lord—ministered with unfailing use of Christ's words of institution and of the elements ordained by Him.

d) The historic episcopate [apostolic succession], locally adapted in the methods of its administration to the varying needs of the nations and peoples called of God into the unity of His church (F. E. Mayer, *The Religious Bodies of America*, 4th ed., revised by Arthur Carl Piepkorn, St. Louis: Concordia, 1961, p. 275).

The Anglican communion, of which the Protestant Episcopal Church of the United States is a part, is a worldwide fellowship, just as the British Empire was once a dominion "on which the sun never set." Thus there are branches of Anglicanism on all continents: Canada, South Africa, India, Australia, New Zealand, Hong Kong, wherever the British flag used to wave. In its total membership the Anglican Communion is the second-largest Protestant church in the world, being outnumbered only by those affiliated with the Lutheran Church. The Protestant Episcopal Church in the United States counts more than 3,000,000 members.

The Episcopal Church feels a strong affinity for the Eastern Orthodox church. It has, in fact, propounded the so-called "branch" theory, which suggests that the churches reaching back beyond the Reformation and having a ministry in unbroken apostolic succession are the legitimate branches of the Catholic Church. Such branches are said to be the Orthodox, the Roman Catholic, the Old Catholic, and the Anglican churches.

The same trends and movements that characterize Anglicanism in Great Britain are discernible within the Episcopal Church in the United States.

Chapter 4

Reformed Churches
of the Calvinist Tradition

After the Thirty Years' War (1618—48) most non-Lutheran Protestant groups were generally called Reformed churches. Their distinctive traits are derived largely from the Swiss Reformation and the theology of Huldreich Zwingli (Zurich, German Switzerland) and especially of John Calvin (Geneva, French Switzerland).

The Reformation in Switzerland began about the time of Luther's work in Germany and was for some time quite independent of it. Zwingli was an ardent patriot who protested against the recruitment of Swiss young men for mercenary service in foreign armies, including the pope's. Zwingli objected to the veneration of relics at a shrine dedicated to Mary in the small town where he served as priest. He was convinced that God did not deal with men through relics or other external means and that the "Holy Spirit needs no vehicle." As a humanist Zwingli was concerned principally with recapturing the life-style of the church before its degeneration through centuries of human traditions and ceremonies. He wanted to reform worship and morals rather than theology, and he strove to achieve it by means of appropriate legislation rather than through the Gospel. His reformation was, on the surface at least, far more radical than Luther's conservative approach. A strong political and social activism characterized his work. Zwingli and Luther met only once. A meeting had been arranged by Philip of Hesse in Marburg, in 1529, with a view to composing the theological differences between these two leaders, so that both the German and the Swiss reformatory movements might present a united front against Rome. The focus of their differences appeared to be divergent views on the nature of Christ and His presence in the Lord's Supper. Luther upheld the "Real Presence" of Christ's body and blood "in, with, and under" the bread and wine, while Zwingli denied it. The latter taught a "spiritual" or symbolic presence. According to his axiom that the "finite cannot contain the infinite," he insisted that it was not possible for the humanity of Christ to be present in more than one place at the same time. No agreement was reached at the Marburg Colloquy, which lasted for several days, and in spite of subsequent attempts down to our own time, Reformed and Lutheran have remained separated ever since.

Zwingli died on a battlefied in 1531 and was succeeded by Henry Bullinger. Some years later the city of Geneva became the center of great reformatory activity under the leadership of John Calvin, a Frenchman who had come to accept the Reformed faith and was exiled from France. Calvin was a man of outstanding intellect and learning, one of the most systematic thinkers of his time. With single-minded devotion he set himself to the task of reforming whatever needed reforming, not only in the church but also in society, in business, and in civil government. Eventually Calvin gained complete control of Geneva and through the city council initiated laws and ordinances regulating all aspects of community life, including commercial and social matters, such as price control and amusements. Geneva became famous as the "Protestant Rome," to which many prominent religious leaders came to seek Calvin's counsel and learn his theology. Calvin's influence reached far beyond Switzerland, and his views gained the support of many thousands in France, western and southern Germany, the Netherlands, and the British Isles, especially Scotland. As emigrants from Great Britain and Holland colonized North America, they brought their Calvinistic theology and ethos with them (predominantly in New England and to a great extent in the middle colonies), and for the greater part of United States history varieties of Calvinism were the dominant factor in shaping American ideas of religion and culture.

Calvin was passionately devoted to the Bible as the precise expression of the will of God, whose absolute sovereignty in all areas of life and whose glorification by every human activity formed the focus of Calvin's existence. To safeguard God's sovereignty Calvin taught that God issued a number of eternal, immutable decrees regarding creation, Christ's work of redemption, and the salvation or damnation of human beings. Predestination was conceived of as twofold, God choosing to save some to glorify His grace and to reprobate or condemn others to glorify His justice.

We call predestination God's eternal decree, by which he determined with himself what he willed to become of each man. For all are not created in equal condition; rather eternal life is fore-ordained for some, eternal damnation for others (John Calvin, Institutes of the Christian Religion, Book III, Chapter

XXI, 5; ed. John T. McNeill, trans. Ford Lewis Battles, in *The Library of Christian Classics*, Vol. XXI, Philadelphia: The Westminster Press, 1960, p. 926).

Calvin's position has perhaps been most closely adopted by the Westminster Confession, the creedal standard of the Presbyterians. Chapter III, Of God's Eternal Decree, states:

> I. God from all eternity did, by the most wise and holy counsel of his own will, freely and unchangeably ordain whatsoever comes to pass; yet so as thereby neither is God the author of sin, nor is violence offered to the will of the creatures, nor is the liberty or contingency of second causes taken away, but rather established.
> III. By the decree of God, for the manifestation of his glory, some men and angels are predestinated unto everlasting life, and others foreordained to everlasting death (The Westminster Confession, in: *Creeds of the Churches*, ed. John H. Leith, Garden City: Anchor Books, 1963, p. 198).

If it were not God's will, so Calvin reasoned, that some should perish, they would not perish, or else God would not be sovereign. Moreover, once God had decreed the salvation of some people, they were bound to be saved, regardless of what they did, or else God would not be sovereign.

Not all creatures were included in God's redemptive plans, but all are held to glorify the sovereign God in their life in whatever way they are able. All men were said to be endowed with "common" grace, enabling them to glorify God on the natural level. Only the "saved" were recipients of "special" grace for salvation.

For Calvin, the church was composed of two distinct groups. All the elect constitute the real church, which is invisible, since no one but God knows who the elect are. All those who are outwardly members of the Christian community are the visible church. Church and state are looked upon as partners in shaping and governing society. Since the Bible speaks of elders in the church, the Biblically prescribed form of church government is said to be presbyterial (from *presbyteros*, the Greek word for elder), with teaching and ruling elders.

A major characteristic of the Calvinistic Reformed tradition is its difference from Roman Catholics and Orthodox, on the one hand, and from Lutherans, on the other, in the doctrine of the sacraments. The

Calvinists fix the number of sacraments at two, Baptism and the Lord's Supper, while Roman Catholics and Orthodox insist on seven, and Lutherans regard the number as a matter of indifference, depending on one's definition of a sacrament (cf. Apology XIII, Tappert, p. 211). For the Reformed, the emphasis lies on the symbolism. They see an extensive parallel between the Old Testament rites of Circumcision and Passover and the sacraments instituted by Christ. Just as circumcision was the outward sign of a child's membership in the chosen people of Israel, so Baptism is the outward sign of membership in the Christian community. Baptism does not bestow regeneration but symbolizes what has happened independent of Baptism by a direct activity of the Holy Spirit. The chief accent appears to be on the action of the Christian community in obedience to Christ's ordinance as an act of public profession that the person being baptized is a member of the community. Just as in the Old Testament the son of an Israelite was an Israelite by birth, so the child of Christian parents is already in the covenant of God's people by birth.

Much the same is true of the Reformed view of the Lord's Supper. The sacrament does not bestow "forgiveness of sins, life, and salvation" (Luther's Small Catechism), but seals and confirms the promise given independently of it. Just as the Passover was a feast of remembrance of God's deliverance, so the Lord's Supper is a memorial of what Christ has done, but it does not convey the gifts He won by His redemptive work. Again, celebrating the Lord's Supper is an act of obedience to the Lord Christ in which the Christian community publicly affirms that the communicants belong to the community. A few citations from leading Reformed confessions will demonstrate where the accent lies.

> These Sacraments, both of the Old Testament and of the New, were instituted by God not only to *make a visible distinction* between his people and those who were without the Covenant, but also to *exercise the faith* of his children and, by participation of these sacraments, to *seal* in their hearts the assurance of his promise ... (The Scottish Confession of Faith, Chapter XXI in Arthur C. Cochrane, *Reformed Confessions of the 16th Century*. Philadelphia: The Westminster Press, 1966, p. 179. Emphases added in this and the following citations).

> [The sacraments] are visible, holy *signs and seals* instituted by God in order that by their use he may the more fully *disclose and seal* to us the promise of the gospel (Heidelberg Catechism, Qu. 66; Cochrane, p. 316).

[The] bread and cup of the Lord ... are given to me as sure *signs* of the body and blood of Christ (Heidelberg Catechism, Qu. 75; Cochrane, p. 316).

Sacraments are holy *signs and seals* of the covenant of grace, immediately instituted by God, to *represent* Christ and his benefits, and to *confirm* our interest in him; as also to put a *visible difference* between those that belong unto the Church, and the rest of the world ... (Westminster Confession, Chapter XXVII; Leith, p. 223).

Baptism is a *sign and seal* of the covenant of grace, of his ingrafting into Christ, of regeneration, of remission of sins, and of his giving up unto God (Westminster Confession, XXVIII; Leith, p. 224).

By way of comparison, note where the Lutheran accents lie.

It is taught among us that the sacraments were instituted not only to be signs by which people might be identified outwardly as Christians, but that they are signs and testimonies of God's will toward us *for the purpose of awakening and strengthening our faith* (Augsburg Confession, XIII; Tappert, p. 35).

It [Baptism] *effects* forgiveness of sins, *delivers* from death and the devil, and *grants* eternal salvation to all who believe, as the Word and promise of God declare (Luther's Small Catechism, IV; Tappert, pp. 348 f.).

Toward forgiveness is directed everything that is to be preached concerning the sacraments and, in short, the entire Gospel and all the duties of Christianity (Luther's Large Catechism, Creed, 54; Tappert, p. 417).

Calvin's emphases were subsequently modified in both directions, either of greater rigor or of greater leniency. A major division in Reformed Protestantism occurred in Holland, in the town of Dort, 1618-1619. Strong opposition to basic principles of Calvinism led to the convening of a Reformed council with a view to settling the controversy. A Dutch theologian by the name of Jacob Hermaans, or Arminius, had vigorously attacked Calvin's theological system, and his supporters were called Arminians. The Arminian attack focussed on five major points of Calvinism, represented by the acrostic t-u-l-i-p:

33

Calvinism	Arminianism
1. Total depravity of man	Man has free will and is capable of cooperating with God
2. Unconditional election	Election conditioned by man's behavior
3. Limited atonement (the elect)	Universal atonement
4. Irresistible grace	Man has power to resist or accept
5. Perseverance in grace	Man can fall away and cannot be certain of his salvation

(cf. Mayer, pp. 225 f.).

Since the Synod of Dort the Reformed family has been divided, and it is proper to speak of Calvinistic Reformed and Arminian Reformed churches.

Among the large number of statements of belief that have sprung from Calvinist Reformed soil those with perhaps the most far-reaching and lasting influence are Calvin's Institutes of the Christian Religion, the Heidelberg Catechism, the Scotch Confession of Faith, and the Westminster Standards. No church body today follows without qualification the doctrinal systems set forth in these documents. Furthermore, because of the large number of Reformed confessions hardly any of them commands the acceptance and commitment of churches in the way the Lutheran Confessions do.

Of current denominations predominantly in the Calvinist tradition we mention the Presbyterians, the Baptists, and the Dutch and German Reformed churches. Since all of these share many of the teachings of the Calvinist tradition, it will not be necessary to discuss them in detail.

A. The Presbyterian Church

Presbyterianism, which claims more than 4,000,000 members in the United States, came to this country from England via Geneva and Scotland. The Scottish clergyman John Knox spent some five years in Geneva with Calvin and absorbed the latter's system. Upon his return to Scotland he succeeded in reforming and organizing the Scottish church according to the Calvinist model and in a matter of days wrote the Scotch Confession of Faith. The Scottish church was in vigorous opposition to Roman Catholicism (Mary, Queen of Scots) on the one hand, and later to the Anglican Church on the other. To the followers of Knox the English church appeared corrupt and still permeated with papist leaven, particularly in the "prelacy," the episcopal system of government. This opposition to the Anglican establishment found expression in a rigorous and ascetic Puritanism, dedicated to purifying church and society.

Puritanism became a powerful factor in 17th-century England and eventually led to the defeat of the forces of the king and his overthrow by Oliver Cromwell. While Cromwell ruled the country as Lord Protector, a reformation of the church along Puritan lines was attempted. Parliament ordered the writing of the Westminster Standards, delineating the beliefs, practices, discipline, and government of the church that were to replace the Anglican model. However, only a few years later the monarchy as well as the Anglican Church were restored, and the influence of Presbyterianism declined in England.

It was quite different in America. Most of the British immigrants in the early stages of colonization were Puritan rather than Anglican, since they were prevented from a free exercise of their religion.

Three-fourths of all American Presbyterians are members of the United Presbyterian Church in the U.S.A. In 1967 the General Assembly adopted a Book of Confessions, a collection of nine creeds, to demonstrate continuity with the ancient church (Nicene Creed, Apostles' Creed), the Reformed tradition (the Scotch Confession, the Heidelberg Catechism, the Second Helvetic Confession, the Westminster Confession and Shorter Catechism, the Theological Declaration of Barmen of 1934), and to give expression to the faith in modern language and thought patterns (The Confession of 1967).

B. Reformed Churches

Several church bodies have the word "Reformed" in their official name. The Reformed Church in America, of Dutch origin, is one of the first Christian groups to appear in America, going back to very early colonial times. Another body of Dutch background is the Christian Reformed Church, with its major strength in Michigan. In addition there are the Hungarian Reformed Church in America, Netherlands Reformed Congregations, Protestant Reformed Churches of America, and Reformed Church in the United States, all of them comparatively small in membership. In general, all of these Reformed churches stand in the tradition of historic Calvinism and follow the basic Calvinistic teachings with slight variations.

35

C. The Baptists

As described by one who is himself a Baptist,

> A Baptist is a faithful follower of Jesus Christ, who sincerely endeavors to establish His way of life among mankind, is a staunch believer in the historic Baptist principle of religious liberty, has been baptized by immersion, and is a member of a parish church which is identified by the name Baptist.
>
> Baptists believe that religion is a personal relationship between the human soul and God. In this realm nothing may intrude—no ecclesiastical system, no governmental regulation, no ordinance, no sacrament, no preacher, no priest. The saving grace of Christ and the infinite mercy of God are available to every individual, without the mediation of any priest or minister or church or system. Baptists believe in the "priesthood of all believers" (William B. Lipphard, "What Is a Baptist?" in Leo Rosten, ed., *Religion in America*. New York: Simon and Schuster, 1963, p. 15).

Baptists claim they project faithfully the image of the New Testament church as founded by Christ Himself. Some see the roots of the Baptist movement in the Anabaptists and Mennonites of the 16th century. More probably it arose somewhat later in England as a part of the Dissenter or Separatist movement. Among the many who were critical of the established church and its hierarchical system there were (1) those who believed the church could be purified from within; they were the Puritans (Presbyterians); (2) those who were convinced the church was beyond reformation and a complete separation was the only way open; these were the "Separatists." These, again, developed into at least two distinct groups, depending upon the degree of their opposition to a superior church government: a) those who believed that each local group of believers (congregation) was fully autonomous, the Congregationalists; b) those who went even farther and insisted that each individual believer is sovereign under the Lord Christ, the Baptists.

The "religious liberty" mentioned in the above statement by William Lipphard is to be taken in its full, comprehensive sense, not only the liberty to practice one's religion without any interference from the civil government, but also liberty for each individual

Christian to believe and practice without any interference from church authorities.

From this basic Baptist concept of the sovereignty of the individual under the lordship of Christ it follows logically that:

1. Every Christian must be free to interpret the Bible for himself.
2. Every Christian must be free to decide for himself with regard to his membership in the church. No superior church government, whether national or local, can prescribe for him or impose its will on him. His participation in the work of the local parish or elsewhere is a voluntary act.
3. No one may dictate his system of belief, his creed, to another. Baptists have historically been opposed to the formulation of official creeds, but that does not mean, of course, that Baptist Christians have no creed; it is that each individual must be allowed to make his statement of belief in his own words.
4. Only those who have already come to faith and desire Baptism for themselves may be baptized; it would be spiritual tyranny to administer Baptism to anyone who objects or to an infant who cannot object.
5. It is more appropriate to speak of Baptist "churches" than of the Baptist "church."

In answer to the question, "Why do Baptists prefer to be called a denomination instead of a church?" Lipphard replies:

> Because most Baptists do not admit that they constitute a "church"—but are organized into local "churches." The local parish church is the sovereign, all-powerful ecclesiastical unit. . . .
>
> Baptists have no hierarchy, no centralized control of religious activity, no headquarters' "oversight" of churches or liturgies, practices or regulations. The local parish church is a law unto itself. Its relations with other churches, its compliance with recommendations from national church headquarters, its acceptance of any resolutions formulated at a convention—all these are entirely voluntary, without the slightest degree of compulsion (Lipphard, pp. 16 f.).

6. There would be a large number of separate and independent groupings of Baptists. This is indeed the case. The approximately 20 million Baptists in the United States are divided into 27

segments. Of these the majority are "particular" or Calvinistic Baptists, while others are more closely associated with Arminian principles and are called "general" Baptists.

7. Every Baptist is a priest before God and must exercise his priesthood by his personal participation in the work and mission of the church.

8. There can really be no authoritative review or control of what Baptists believe and teach, and since there are no official statements of belief, there can, strictly speaking, be no "false" teaching. Both extreme conservatism and extreme liberalism, as well as all shades in between, may be found, and found legitimately, in Baptist churches.

Chapter 5

Reformed Churches of the Arminian Tradition

Calvinism, as was shown earlier, placed strong emphasis on God's absolute sovereignty, as expressed in His eternal, immutable decrees, and on man's corresponding complete subjection to God's sovereign will in all areas of life. In this scheme God's unconditional decree of election, or predestination, and the resulting concept of a limited atonement played a considerable role. We recall that these teachings were vigorously opposed within Reformed circles by the Dutch theologian Jacob Arminius and his followers, called Arminians. From its beginning early in the 17th century Arminianism has grown to become a major force within the Reformed tradition. The principal church groups to spring from the Arminian theology are the Methodists, the Holiness groups, the Salvation Army, and related organizations.

Reduced to its simplest terms, where Calvinism stressed a theology centering in God and His will and His deeds, Arminianism shifted the focus to man, giving prominence to man's native ability, man's free will, man's deeds, man's inner feelings. In varying degrees these accents may be discerned in all the members of the Arminian family.

A. The Methodist Church

Methodism owes its origin, development, and ultimate direction largely to the character, efforts, and influence of one man, John Wesley, the third great Protestant leader, next to Luther and Calvin.

The great movement inaugurated by Wesley was principally by way of reaction to a specific set of historical circumstances in England. In the 16th century, under Queen Elizabeth I, the Church of England was established, flexible enough in its theology, it was hoped, to permit a variety of Christians to get along in one national church. In the 17th century, as we heard, an attempt originating in Calvinist

Scotland was made to reform or "purify" the church from within. This endeavor led to the production of the Westminster Standards of the Presbyterian Church. As we know, this had no lasting effect. The Establishment, consisting of the Crown, the church, the nobility, the Tory press, and the social and economic upper class, regained control. Subsequently Deism (belief in the existence of an impersonal "Supreme Being") and rationalism (rejecting what cannot be harmonized with reason) infiltrated the theology of the church and robbed the Christian message of much of its basic content. The church became identified with the privileged class and appeared to have little to offer the great masses of the poor and underprivileged. The liturgical rubrics and forms of the Book of Common Prayer were generally observed as the clergy went through the motions of worship, but there seemed to be no life in it.

To these conditions of economic inequity and exploitation, of social discrimination, and of religious smugness, doctrinal erosion, and cold formalism John Wesley, his brother Charles, and others in their circle, reacted. In some respects it was much like the situation in German Lutheranism, where Orthodoxy, expending its energies to a large extent in harping on correct theological formulas and in endless attacks on those who deviated from them, had lost the interest and loyalty of the masses. These were repelled by what seemed to them dry-as-dust theologizing that took the heart out of religion, and their reaction was the movement within the church known as Pietism.

Similar circumstances led to similar reactions in England. This was the great experience of the church in 18th-century England. The Wesley brothers were ordained clergymen of the Church of England and had no desire to separate themselves from it. Unlike the Presbyterians, who believed that the church's episcopal system of government needed to be changed, and unlike the Congregationalists and Baptists who were convinced that their only course was separation, Wesley and his followers were quite content with the church's governmental structure. All they wanted was to revitalize the nation's religion, stimulate a genuine heartfelt faith, and induce the people to lead sanctified lives.

The Wesleys came to their ideas early in life. They were reared in a very large parsonage family, where sheer necessity compelled the gifted and resourceful mother to adopt rules and regulations for the maintenance of domestic order. At Oxford University the Wesleys were appalled by the worldliness of the students and determined to counteract it by strict methods of Bible study, prayer, and admonition. In derision their fellow students called this group "Holy Club" or

"Methodists." The basic elements of Wesley's system were the attainment of holiness, or perfection, or entire sanctification, through methodical observance of rules and regulations under the supervision of other Christians. The Methodist Book of Discipline, Par. 92, describes the organization as

> a company of men having the form and seeking the power of godliness, united in order to pray together, to receive the work of exhortation, and to watch over one another in love, that they may help each other work out their salvation.

For Wesley the principal concern was life rather than doctrine, and therefore the movement has always been prominent in social activity. Wesley himself describes a Methodist as

> one who lives according to the method laid down in the Bible; who loves the Lord with all his heart and prays without ceasing; whose heart is full of love toward all mankind and is purified from envy, malice, wrath and every unkind affection; who keeps all God's commandments from the least unto the greatest; who follows not the customs of the world; who cannot speak evil of his neighbor any more than he can lie; who does good to all men. . . . These are the marks of a Methodist. By these alone do Methodists desire to be distinguished from other men (cited in the *Christian Advocate*, May 19, 1938).

The following estimate of the Methodist Church suggests commitment to basic Arminian principles, as outlined earlier:

> In many ways it is our most characteristic church. It is short on theology, long on good works, brilliantly organized, primarily middle-class, frequently bigoted, incurably optimistic, zealously missionary, and touchingly confident of the essential goodness of the man next door (Editorial in *Life*, November 19, 1947).

While the more than 14 million American Methodists are affiliated with more than 20 separate bodies, the vast majority are members of the United Methodist Church, established in 1968 as the result of several mergers.

41

B. Holiness Bodies

The Wesleyan movement arose within the Church of England as a protest against the cold formalism of the church and the moral laxity of the people, with no intention of separating from the church. It was only after the established church would not tolerate their activities that the followers of Wesley formed the Methodist Church as a distinct denomination.

Eventually Methodism became a large and powerful and "respectable" church, fully accepted by the established Protestant community. The church was no longer a militant protest movement, and very much of the original crusading zeal ebbed away. This situation led to a reaction within the denomination in protest against the cooling of Methodist ardor for sanctification. Thus the Holiness movement was born. The demand for complete, unqualified holiness of life was made the central doctrinal concern. When the organized church would not tolerate what it regarded as excesses in the movement, the protestors withdrew and formed their own organizations. Typical of their position is the doctrinal statement of the Church of the Nazarene, the largest organized body among Holiness, or perfectionist, groups:

> We deem belief in the following sufficient: (1) in one God, the Father, Son, and Holy Ghost; (2) in the plenary inspiration of the Old and New Testaments; (3) that man is born with a fallen nature and is therefore inclined to evil, and that continually; (4) that the finally impenitent are hopelessly and eternally lost; (5) that the atonement through Jesus is for the whole human race and that whoever repents and believes on the Lord Jesus Christ is justified and regenerated and saved from the dominion of sin; (6) that the believers are to be *sanctified wholly* (emphasis added), subsequent to regeneration through faith in the Lord Jesus; (7) that *the Holy Spirit bears witness to the new birth and also to entire sanctification of believers* (emphasis added); (8) in the return of our Lord, in the resurrection of the dead, and in the final judgment (Manual of the History, Doctrine, Government and Ritual of the Church of the Nazarene, cited in Mayer, pp. 309 f.).

According to the Scriptures it is the Holy Spirit who creates faith and produces the holy life. Therefore the Holy Spirit is very prominent in Holiness teaching. The "baptism with the Holy Spirit" produces "born again" Christians, who are transformed instantly into a state where they no longer commit a willful sin and are therefore entirely sanctified. Such imperfections as remain, it is claimed, do not come from inner promptings of the heart but are stimulations coming from outside. Justification is said to provide forgiveness for sins actually committed, while sanctification is alleged to remove original, or "inbred," sin, a condition involving no guilt. Remembering the Arminian emphasis on free will and man's less than total depravity after the Fall, it is only consistent for Holiness people to believe that since God demands holiness, it must be in man's power to achieve it even in this life.

Other Holiness bodies are a number of groups named Church of God, the Christian and Missionary Alliance, and various smaller organizations.

C. Pentecostals

Another group of churches within the Methodist family quite closely related to the Holiness churches are the Pentecostals. As the name implies, the outpouring of the Holy Spirit at the first Pentecost is in the center of their teaching. But while the Holiness groups emphasize the work of the Holy Spirit in entire sanctification, the Pentecostals lay stress on the miraculous, the charismatic gifts of the Holy Spirit. The Constitution of the Pentecostal Fellowship of North America affirms, in addition to basic beliefs as summarized in the ancient Christian creeds:

(5) that the full gospel includes holiness of heart and life, *healing for the body and the baptism in the Holy Spirit with the initial evidence of speaking in other tongues as the Spirit gives utterance* (emphasis added; cited in Mayer, p. 310).

Pentecostals regard "baptism in the Holy Spirit" as far more important and effective than the water Baptism instituted by Christ. Baptism in the Spirit is said to endow those Christians fortunate enough to receive it with extra gifts not experienced by "ordinary" Christians. Many Pentecostals believe that the "full Gospel" includes four aspects, the "Gospel Foursquare": Christ the Savior, the Sanctifier, the Healer, and the Coming King. The last one refers to belief in Christ's return to this earth to establish the millennium.

There are a number of Pentecostal churches, some containing the word "Pentecostal" in their name, while others call themselves Assemblies of God, or Churches of God. Formerly the Pentecostals or

"Charismatics" were not welcome in old-line churches, and for that reason they formed separate groups. In recent times, however, they have appeared in most of the churches, Roman Catholic, Episcopalian, Lutheran, etc., as forces to be reckoned with, at times even hailed as resources for revitalizing a Christianity that seems to have gone flat. This development is sometimes referred to as Neo-Pentecostalism.

D. Related Bodies

Other churches in the larger Methodist family include the Evangelical United Brethren Church, a merger of two former German Methodist groups and now part of the United Methodist Church, and the Salvation Army. The latter, organized in 1878 by William Booth in England, is usually thought of more often as an agency for social service than as a church, although its religious principles are much like those of Welsey and the Holiness groups. The central theme of the Salvation Army is holiness of life. This concern finds its strongest expression in the attempts to rehabilitate the down-and-outer and rebuild his character. The humanitarian and philanthropic activities of the Salvation Army are widely recognized.

Chapter 6

Attempts at Overcoming Denominationalism

Since the days of the apostles there have been differences among Christians in their understanding and teaching of Christian doctrine and its implications for the Christian life. Likewise, since the beginning of the church these differences have been deplored and efforts were put forth to remove them, correct erroneous teaching, overcome separations resulting from these differences, and thus restore unity to those who bear the Christian name. The apostle St. Paul writes pastor Titus that the spiritual leader must be a person of firm convictions, "so that he may be able to give instruction in sound doctrine and also to confute those who contradict it" (Titus 1:9). Writing to young pastor Timothy, St. Paul speaks of "stupid, senseless controversies" that "breed quarrels" (2 Timothy 2:23). "The Lord's servant," he says, "must not be quarrelsome," but one "correcting his opponents with gentleness" (vv. 24, 25). With great solemnity the old apostle charges Timothy to "preach the Word, . . . convince, rebuke, and exhort, . . . For the time is coming when people will not endure sound teaching, . . . and will turn away from listening to the truth." (2 Timothy 4:1-4).

In the early centuries following the apostolic age, when controversy and heresy regarding matters of faith or life threatened to produce strife and disunity, the leaders of the church were summoned to councils and charged to take measures to overcome the difficulties, affirm the truth, and reject false teaching. In spite of some partial successes in healing schisms in the church, the long history of Christianity is more often than not a record of human frailty and perversity and failure to "keep the unity of the Spirit." Even during the Middle Ages, when the Roman Catholic Church appeared to present a united front throughout western and northern Europe, there were ever recurring conflicts with, and dissent from, the church's official position in doctrine or practice. Since the Reformation, with its emphasis on the freedom of conscience and the right of private judgment, there have been a number of divisions, persisting to the present day and even increasing.

Yet the 19th and 20th centuries witnessed indications of a reversal of this trend to multiply separation and some attempts to reunite what had been separate for so long. Earlier in the church's history differences in the church were often dealt with by forcible suppression of both the dissent and the dissenters. In fact, this method was responsible to a considerable degree for the emigration of many hundreds of thousands of Christians from various European countries and their quest for religious liberty in America. Even here, in early colonial history, nonconformists were often subjected to civil penalties, imprisonment, and even exile.

But now the problem of a divided Christendom was to be approached in a different way, with no further discrimination and persecution. Basically there were and are three ways of dealing with the problem:

1) Recognize the differences among churches but regard them as nondivisive and establish a common doctrinal denominator. On this basis a number of churches of similar ethnic, cultural, and religious background might merge into one and thus help overcome denominationalism.

2) Repudiate all aspects of denominationalism, such as distinctive names and teachings, discard the accumulated materials of the theological language, creedal statements, liturgies, and so forth, roll back the centuries, and restore the church to what it was in the New Testament.

3) Recognize and deplore all differences based on false teaching and strive to overcome them by patient doctrinal dialog, being careful to observe the distinction between theological and nontheological factors, between things that are truly divisive and those that are not, or need not be.

Of these three options the first one was chosen by the United Church of Christ, the second by the Disciples, and the third has been and is being employed by various churches, including the Lutheran.

A. The United Church of Christ

Although this merger took place as recently as 1957, the churches that formed it reach back a number of centuries. There have been earlier mergers, of course, but they were composed of churches of the same cultural and theological background and with the same form of church government (polity). The United Church of Christ, however, combined churches of both English and German background, of Calvinistic and Lutheran roots, and of dissimilar forms of church government. The merger united the General Council of Congregational and Christian Churches (itself a merger) with the Evangelical and Reformed Church (also a merger). Of this union Douglas Horton, a distinguished scholar and member, wrote:

> We are separated by more than basic belief. For one thing, denominations contemplating union need to come to know, to understand, and finally to appreciate each other in the apparently untheological human category of cultural customs. In every proposed church union, sociological forces pent in the group mind come out. In the union of the Congregational Christian with the Evangelical and Reformed Churches, the New England boiled dinner and Pennsylvania sauerkraut had to come to terms with each other: the culinary differences had their place with the theological (Douglas Horton, *The United Church of Christ*, New York: Thomas Nelson & Sons, 1962, pp. 20 f.).

The Congregationalists were Calvinists who in 17th-century England dissented from, and were bitterly opposed to, the episcopal polity of the Church of England. As the name implies, they believed that each local community of Christians must be free to govern its own affairs. For their refusal to conform, they were harshly dealt with, and they escaped to America. Here they colonized and gained massive control over most of New England. They were generally called Puritans. With a one-sided emphasis on the sovereignty of each congregation, there was no effective oversight of doctrine. As a result, a large number of Congregationalist churches became Unitarian, especially in eastern Massachusetts.

Several other groups with roots in New England and of Methodist, Baptist, and Unitarian backgrounds, protesting what was regarded as interference with individual freedom in the church, eventually brought about the formation of churches calling themselves "Christian." They formulated no theological basis of their belief and teaching, and the only test of membership was "Christian character." With these churches the Congregationalists united in 1931 to form the General Council of Congregational and Christian Churches.

The other major component of the United Church of Christ is the Evangelical and Reformed Church, made up of the former Evangelical Synod and the Reformed Church. The Evangelical Synod itself represents a fusion of Lutheran and Reformed elements in Germany, brought about by the decree of Frederick William III of Prussia in 1817, the 300th anniversary of the Reformation, compelling the union of Lutheran and Reformed churches in the so-called Prussian Union. The Reformed Church in the United States stems from the German Reformed Church, an attempt to combine Lutheran and Calvinist elements while avoiding what were regarded as the extremes of either. These two groups of German background merged in 1934 to form the Evangelical and Reformed Church. This church, in turn, merged with the Congregational Christian churches to form the United Church of Christ.

Because of many diverse doctrinal elements coming together in this union, there is little stress on confessional formulations. At its first General Synod in 1959 the United Church of Christ adopted this Statement of Faith:

We believe in God, the Eternal Spirit, Father of our Lord Jesus Christ and our Father, and to his deeds we testify:

He calls the worlds into being, creates man in his own image and sets before him the ways of life and death.

He seeks in holy love to save all people from aimlessness and sin.

He judges men and nations by his righteous will declared through prophets and apostles.

In Jesus Christ, the man of Nazareth, our crucified and risen Lord, he has come to us and shared out common lot, conquering sin and death and reconciling the world to himself.

He bestows upon us his Holy Spirit, creating and renewing the Church of Jesus Christ, binding in covenant faithful people of all ages, tongues, and races.

He calls us into his Church to accept the cost and joy of discipleship, to be his servants in the service of men, to proclaim the gospel to all the world and resist the powers of evil, to share in Christ's baptism and eat at his table, to join him in his passion and victory.

He promises to all who trust him forgiveness of sins and fullness of grace, courage in the struggle for justice and peace, his presence in trial and rejoicing, and eternal life in his kingdom which has no end.

Blessing and honor, glory and power be unto him. Amen (Horton, p. 66).

Even this is only "a testimony rather than a test of faith," and as such it is not binding upon anyone.

B. The Disciples of Christ

While the United Church of Christ is an attempt to overcome denominationalism by way of merger, the Disciples opted for the second approach mentioned above, namely discarding the historical denominations altogether and going back to the New Testament. Since this approach endeavors to "restore" the church to its original stature, this movement has been given the overall name of "restorationism."

While this movement was developed and promoted by men of Reformed background, Congregationalist, Presbyterian, Baptist, and Methodist, and is thus in the Protestant Christian tradition, it is largely a product of conditions in America with its heady experience of complete religious liberty and individualism especially evident on the frontier.

Around 1800 the frontier was in western Pennsylvania, eastern Ohio, Kentucky, and Tennessee. People of many diverse cultural, educational, political, economic, and religious backgrounds populated the frontier and devoted themselves to the difficult task of wresting a living from the wilderness and protecting their families from hostile attacks by Indians and from other hardships. In such a setting the preservation and promotion of separate denominational groups seemed to many people a luxury they could no longer afford. Having made common cause with their neighbors in all phases of the work and worry on the frontier, they were ready to do their worshiping together also.

The soil was prepared for the "Restoration Movement," which had its beginning some years earlier. The leaders in western Pennsylvania were Thomas Campbell and his son, Alexander, of Scottish Presbyterian background. It was particularly Alexander, a highly gifted man, who crystalized the principles of this movement and gave it its ultimate direction. For that reason the churches resulting from his work were at first often called "Campbellites," a label which these groups repudiate.

The Campbells and others were foes of all denominational names and teachings. They felt that every denominational creed was a barrier to Christian unity. All labels and theological terms not found in the New Testament were to be discarded. Since the New Testament knows of no Catholic, or Lutheran, or Presbyterian Church, or any of the others, church members should use Biblical titles exclusively, above all, Disciple, or Christian. At the same time, the Disciples are opposed to any formulated creeds or statements of doctrine. They claim to "have no creed but Christ," and to be "God-centered, Christ-centered, Bible-centered, with no creed save one—the answer of the apostle Peter to a question from Jesus himself: 'Thou art the Christ, the Son of the Living God'" (James E. Craig, "Who Are the Disciples of Christ?" in Rosten, p. 58).

The rich and unbelievable value of the simplicity of our confession of faith is made clear when we turn to the innumerable creeds of Christendom. Each one of these contains much worth-while Christian truth and embodies deep and vital convictions of godly men. Even so, *creeds come between us and Christ.* In accepting a creed, we accept other people's interpretations of Christ. These interpretations may be in interesting, true or false, but we are not saved by interpretations. We are saved by Christ and by him only.

Again, if creeds come between us and Christ, *they come also between us and other Christians.* If our confession of faith were a creed with its many truths and omissions, we would be fenced off from other Christians holding different creeds. When we have "no creed but Christ," we have no such barriers (H. B. McCormick, *Our Confession of Faith,* Prepared by Home and States Missions Planning Council, Disciples of Christ. Published by the United Christian Missionary Society, Indianapolis, Indiana, p. 5 f., emphases added).

To the question, How do the Disciples differ from other Protestants? James E. Craig, a prominent Disciple, answers, among other things:

They regard conversion as a voluntary, rational act which does not require special personal revelation. In receiving a new member . . . they employ no formula of interrogation . . .

They admit to the Lord's Supper any baptized person, without regard to his sectarian affiliations.

Perhaps the most notable difference between Disciples and other Protestant groups is the emphasis of Disciples upon individual liberty of opinion, upon the right of each man to interpret the Scriptures in his own way.

. . . .

They hold that as long as a member accepts the simple faith, and the idea of democratic government in the church, he may believe what his mind dictates about many of the tenets of other Christian bodies.

Disciples observe with joy that the differences among Protestants are receiving less and less attention today, while the many things they have in common receive more and more. To Disciples, the rising trend towards a mutual ground of faith marks a steady advance toward ultimate church unity. And in this field the Disciples have made their influence most heavily felt. They have been in the forefront of almost every important Protestant cooperative and ecumenical movement (Rosten, p. 65).

Local groups are usually called "Christian Church," or "Church of Christ," while the official corporate name is the "International Convention of Christian Churches (Disciples of Christ)." Membership totals are well above one and one half million.

C. The Moravians

The Moravian Church is the oldest among union churches. As the name suggests, it originated in Moravia, a section of what is now Czechoslovakia, as a result of the teaching of John Huss and Jerome of Prague early in the 15th century. The movement arose in protest against the formalism of the church's worship and creeds, and it emphasized life rather than doctrine. In the Reformation age during the 16th century the Moravians inclined toward Reformed teaching rather than Lutheran. They called themselves *Unitas Fratrum* (Unity of the Brethren). Almost completely annihilated during the Roman Catholic Counter-Reformation, this brotherhood was revived early in the 18th century and given asylum on the estate of Count Zinzendorf in Saxony. From there they unfolded a strong missionary activity and reached out to America and other lands. Though counting only some 60,000 members, the Moravians to the present day have an active missionary program. Their principal stress is on what Christians have in common and on personal piety. Their slogan is "In essentials unity, in nonessentials liberty, in all things charity."

D. The United Church of Canada

In 1925 most Canadian Methodist and Congregationalist churches, plus a number of Presbyterians, joined forces to form the United Church of Canada. The Anglicans of Canada declined to enter the merger because of their stand on the office of the ministry and on church government, while the Baptists remained outside because of their opposition to any organization beyond the local level. In order to achieve a union of churches of both Calvinist and Arminian traditions, the United Church has skirted controversial points of doctrine or resorted to formulations that could be interpreted in more than one way.

Chapter 7

The Inner Light

Throughout the history of the Christian church there have been individuals and movements that expected and claimed to have experienced direct contact or communication with God. Some believed that by certain forms of meditation and spiritual exercise they could lift up their soul and unite it with God. This is usually called Mysticism and is often associated with far Eastern religions, but taking a different form within the framework of Christianity. Other people affirmed that God, especially the Holy Spirit, in some way came directly into their soul and endowed them with the will and the energy to lead a Christian life. They alleged that the sovereign Holy Spirit had the power to achieve His work in men's hearts without resorting to external means or "vehicles," like the Word of God and the sacraments. This view of the Holy Spirit's activity is usually called Enthusiasm. Many Christian theologians who advocated some such idea were not entirely consistent and continued to make use of the external means of preaching and offering the sacraments for the faith and life of the people. Some, however, proceeded from the premise of God's direct spiritual activity to the logical conclusion of using no means at all, or of using them only to verify what they believed God was saying to them directly.

This more extreme form of Enthusiasm is variously called Inner Light, Inner Voice, Spiritual Illumination, or Divine Immanence, the presence of God within the heart. During the Reformation in the 16th century such views were propounded mainly by the so-called Anabaptists, who rejected infant baptism and inisted on rebaptizing those baptized as infants (hence Ana-baptists, re-baptizers). They stressed a religion of inwardness and withdrawal from affairs of the world.

A. The Mennonites

The Anabaptists were severely persecuted and scattered. The remnants were gathered and organized by one Menno Simons, a former Roman Catholic priest. He received rebaptism and soon became the leader of the movement, with the result that his followers were called Mennonites. Leaving Switzerland and Holland, many of them settled in Southern Russia and Germany, from where they came to America and established their colonies in Pennsylvania, Ohio, Indiana, South Dakota, and other states.

Mennonites believe that

> Christ must be known and believed according to the spirit in His exaltation . . . so that *the form and image of Christ is developed in us*, that He manifests Himself to us, dwells in us, teaches us, completes the miracles in us according to the spirit which He performed while in the flesh, heals us of the sickness of our spirit, blindness, impurity, sin, and death, nourishes us with heavenly food, and *makes us partakers of His divine nature*, so that by His power the old man in us is crucified and we arise to a new life, experiencing the power of His resurrection (From the *Confessio Brevis* of 1580, cited in Mayer, p. 401, all emphases added).

Through this mystical experience of Christ the Christian is said to be able to understand the Bible, which otherwise would remain a dark book. Mennonites strongly emphasize the requirement of outward holiness in the church, withdrawal from the world, and a life of simplicity and self-denial. Consequently there is a highly developed system of discipline, a set of laws to safeguard the purity of the fellowship and to exclude the offender. The Gospel is called "the law of Christ in which the whole counsel and will of God are comprehended." In essence the Mennonite way of salvation is linked to the personal piety of the member through his mystical union with Christ. Hence salvation appears not so much as being received through faith in the Christ *for* us as rather through the experience of the Christ *in* us.

Because they believe that Christ comes to dwell in their hearts directly, Mennonites do not regard Gospel and sacraments as means of grace, as the instruments through which the Holy Spirit creates and sustains the spiritual life, but they see in the sacraments nothing more than symbols. Baptism is merely the outward sign that a person has already been united with Christ, and it can therefore be given only to an adult. The Lord's Supper is only a reminder of Christ's death and an exhortation to mutual love. Many Mennonites observe footwashing as a symbol of humility and spiritual purification.

Not all Mennonites have the same view of what constitutes piety and aloofness from the things of this world. Many members were charged with laxity in their Christian life. The leader of this protest was a Swiss layman named Jacob Amman, or Amen. His followers were called "Amish." Historically, Mennonites have placed more emphasis on life than on doctrine. They are advocates of nonresistance, refusal to take oaths before magistrates, as well as opposition to lawsuits and the use of force. They also forbid or discourage the use of all forms of luxury and appliances that may be considered "worldly." Conservative Amish still reject the use of electricity and automobiles, continuing to use horse and buggy on modern highways and candles or coal-oil lanterns instead. In general, Mennonites of various kinds, numbering some 100,000 in the United States, are known as honest, hardworking, law-abiding citizens.

B. The Quakers

Another body characterized by inwardness and giving even more complete expression to it than Mennonites is the Religious Society of Friends, commonly known as Quakers. They may well be the most protestant movement in Protestantism, for they have pushed the principle of direct communication from God forward more consistently than anyone else.

The founder of this movement was George Fox in 17th-century England. He was deeply disturbed by the extremely low ebb of religious life, the moral laxity of many clergymen, the brutalities of the civil war between the forces of King Charles I and of Cromwell, and man's inhumanity to man in general. He claimed that a voice within him told him: "There is one, even Jesus Christ, that can speak to thy condition."

This is the Inner Voice, or Inner Light, which Fox believed was God's way of speaking directly to all human beings, indeed, of dwelling in all people, quite apart from any outward Word of God. Quakers think that John 1:9, "the true Light which lights every man that comes into the world," speaks to this situation. With Fox they affirm that there is "that of God" in every man. This may be defined as divine immanence, God already present within every person, the exact opposite of divine transcendence, which teaches that God is so far removed from His creatures that there is no contact or communication at all.

To the question of how Quakers rate themselves in relation to other Christians, the answer is:

Quakers consider themselves a "third way" of Christians' emphasizing fundamentals differently from Roman Catholics

55

and Protestants. Roman Catholics emphasize church authority, the hierarchy, and an absolute creed. Protestant denominations emphasize one or another interpretation of religion as found in the Holy Bible. But the Society of Friends puts its mark on religion as a fellowship of the Spirit, a movement which can and does grow, develop, and change because it has within it the inward power of expansion. To Friends, all those who do the will of the Father are brethren of Jesus in the Spirit (Richmond P. Miller, "What Is a Quaker?" in Rosten, p. 165).

The basic Quaker beliefs are described as follows:

The faith of a Friend is simple and rests on absolute sincerity. Quakers believe that God can be approached and experienced by the individual directly—without any intermediary priest or preacher. God is experienced through the "Inward Light," which is the spirit of "Christ Within." From this contact, God's will is determined, direction is given for all human affairs, and the power to live the abundant life is shared (ibid.).

The "Inward Light" is not conscience. It is what Quakers call "that of God" in every man. It instructs and transforms the conscience as the true guide of life. Most often it is termed the "Inner Light" or the "Light Within." It exists in all men and women.... For Friends, it is the source of all reality in religion, leading immediately to the experience of God (ibid. p. 165 f.).

The Quaker premise of the presence of the divine in every human being has logically found expression in a number of ways:

1. Since God is already present within, no means are required to bring Him in from without. Therefore there is no need of the clergy, of preaching and the sacraments, and of churches (called "steeple-'houses"). Quakers do have a "Meeting for Worship," but it is a gathering "on the basis of silence." Anyone of the attendants may be moved to break the silence by a prayer, Bible reading, or some spiritual message. There is no prearranged order of service. Quakers do not practice water baptism and do not celebrate the Holy Communion.

2. Since there is "that of God" in every person, everyone is clothed with a high dignity, and nothing dare be done with or to another human being to degrade or debase him. This is the basis of the world-renowned Quaker humanitarianism. There must be no distinction in

rank, no slavery, war, discrimination, capital punishment, inhumane treatment of the mentally ill, no taking of oaths. Quakers have been in the forefront of endeavors for social betterment.

3. Since God dwells within every human being, Quakers have a very high view of man's inborn goodness and are inclined to minimize the seriousness of sin.

The Quakers believe that while sin is a fact in life, it is best described as existing in a universe like a checkerboard of black (sin) and white (goodness) squares. But the black squares are imposed on the basic white squares, not the reverse. There is "an ocean of light over the ocean of darkness" George Fox said. To Friends, the term "original sin" overemphasizes the power of evil. Even when he is fallen, man still belongs to God, who continues to appeal to the goodness within him (Rosten, p. 171).

The Society of Friends numbers some 125,000 members in the United States, many of them in Pennsylvania, where in colonial times William Penn, himself a Quaker, granted the Quakers asylum.

C. The Amana Church Society

A small religious group numbering less than 1,000 adherents, the Amana Society deserves notice because of its unique experiment with Christian communism.

This movement began in western Germany early in the 18th century, much like Pietism in protest against what was regarded as the cold formalism of the Lutheran Church. Supporters of the movement believed that God spoke to their leaders (John Rock and Eberhard Gruber) directly and are thus related at this point to the Mennonites and Quakers. They called themselves the Community of True Inspiration, claiming direct revelation and inspiration from God. After some initial success the movement declined, since the revelations appeared to have come to an end.

Early in the 19th century Christian Metz and Barbara Heinemann Landmann revived the claim. Metz set out to bring all his followers together in one community where all the members might lead the simple life and have all their goods in common. Since this ideal could not be realized in Germany, the society came to America and settled near Buffalo, New York.

When they outgrew their estate, they bought a large tract of land near Iowa City and established a number of small communities. This settlement was called Amana, "Remain True." Here the society has lived ever since. Originally all affairs, spiritual and secular, were under single control, but since 1932 the Amana Society handles all civil, business, and commercial affairs, while all matters pertaining to the church were assigned to the Amana Church Society. "Amana" has become a household word wherever Amana refrigerators and freezers are in use. Other fine Amana products include woolens and hand-crafted furniture.

In addition to basic Christian, Trinitarian beliefs which the Amana people share, they also teach that the Holy Spirit

> even now speaks and operates audibly through the instruments of true inspiration, and hidden inwardly, through the heart and conscience towards repentance and renewal of heart . . . *(A Brief History of the Amana Society.* Amana, Iowa, 1918, cited in Mayer, p. 423).

They do not administer water baptism but believe in a "baptism by fire and the Spirit." There is almost no observance of Holy Communion.

Chapter 8

The Millennium

Ever since the fall into sin and the loss of paradise, as well as because of the experience of all the ills resulting from sin, mankind has yearned for a paradise regained. Amid the cruelties and inequities, the injustices and woes of this life, whether personal or national, people have longed for a time when all evil would be overcome and all evildoers destroyed, so that nothing but perfect bliss would reign. And indeed, God has made provision for redemption, reconciliation, and restoration, moved by His love and mercy, and made a reality through the life and death and resurrection of His Son, Jesus Christ. Forgiveness of sins, life, and salvation are God's gracious gifts to His fallen creatures. Through prophecies and promises God nourished the faith and hope of His people from generation to generation. The gracious reign of God in the hearts and lives of people in a coming age was pictured in glowing colors and gorgeous images and exquisite poetry. A correct interpretation of these pictures was, of course, very important.

Unfortunately, the interpretation on the part of both Christians and Jews was often quite mistaken and led to fanciful dreams of a golden age, a utopia, a never-never land, a bright tomorrow, a glorious time of one thousand years (millennium), and a new heaven on earth. Jewish ideas of the golden age were strongly influenced by the teachings of the Persian Zoroaster, which the Jews learned to know during their captivity in Babylon. Having lost their independence and being subjected to oppression by the Babylonians, Persians, Egyptians, Greeks, and finally the Romans, the Jews longed for an earthly deliverance and a restoration of the glorious kingdom of David. Their interpretation of the picturesque prophecies of the new age and of the Messiah was adapted to conform to their hopes. Even the disciples and followers of Jesus entertained some of these ideas and looked for an earthly kingdom of glory. The mother of James and John requested of Jesus that her two sons "may sit, one at Your right hand and one at Your left, in Your kingdom" (Matthew 20:21). Even after the Lord's resurrection the disciples were still asking, "Lord, will You at this time restore the kingdom to Israel?" (Acts 1:6). The early

59

Christians took over elements of the Jewish hopes of a millennium and attempted to fit them into the framework of the Christian message.

In the course of His discourses to His disciples Jesus made repeated reference to the end of this present world and His return in glory at that time for the purpose of executing a universal judgment. At the Lord's ascension the angelic messengers told the disciples, "This Jesus, who was taken up from you into heaven, will come in the same way as you saw Him go into heaven" (Acts 1:11). This return of Christ at the end is called His second Advent and it constitutes the final act of the story of salvation as summarized in all ancient Christian creeds: "From thence He shall come to judge the quick and the dead." The technical theological term for the teachings concerning the "last things" is eschatology (from the Greek *eschaton*, meaning "last"). It is therefore quite natural that the apostles in their preaching and letters to the churches should often remind the Christians of their eschatological hope and ultimate destiny in the light of Christ's second advent. It was therefore also to be expected that Christians from the beginning nurtured their faith and bolstered their courage by remembering the promises about the future, particularly in times of great calamity, such as widespread oppression and persecution.

The way Christians interpreted and applied the Biblical passages dealing with the end, especially the degree to which their emphasis was predominantly either this-worldly or other-worldly, either physical or spiritual, determined whether their eschatology was regarded as orthodox or heretical. In the early centuries a number of theologians were explicitly chiliastic (Greek: *chilias*, one thousand, cf. Revelation 20:1-7; chiliasm means exactly the same as millennialism, which derives from the Latin for 1000 years). However, by the end of the fourth century most forms of chiliasm had been condemned by the church as unbiblical. When generations passed without Christ's return and when Christianity became the accepted religion, longing for that future golden age seemed to decrease or even to be regarded as being in process of fulfillment.

Within the last 150 years or so there has been a strong revival of chiliastic hopes and teaching. A number of factors have contributed to this resurgence. As private Bible study and interpretation was encouraged, many of the Christian laity discovered the wealth of poetic and highly figurative sections in the writings of some of the Old Testament prophets, such as Isaiah, Ezekiel, Daniel, and others, and in the New Testament book of Revelation, and took them quite literally. Furthermore, recent eras of church history have witnessed the rise of science and interest in this world and material things, with a corresponding drop in concern for the things of the world to come. Many looked upon this universe as closed and self-sufficient, and regarded the Bible's message concerning the end of this world and its final judgment by a returning Christ with increasing skepticism. The kingdom of God, the golden age, they said, was not something to look forward to, but was being realized here and now in a general betterment of the human condition. In reaction to this deemphasis of eschatology, many conservative Christians began to give special emphasis to this area of the faith and even placed it into the center of their message. Major catastrophes in our century, particularly the two World Wars and the the tensions between the free world and the nations under dictatorships, have heightened concern for an ultimate deliverance. Last but not least, the establishment of the state of Israel in the ancestral land of Palestine has contributed greatly to a renewed interest in what Biblical prophecy might be saying about the future of Israel.

Generally millennialism is not confined to specific denominations but often spreads to a greater or lesser degree across a number of denominational lines, being prominent in many Holiness and Pentecostal churches as well as in Baptist and fundamentalist-literalist traditions. All chiliasts believe that Christ's second advent will be associated with a visible, physical kingdom on earth, but there is considerable difference in details. Some maintain that Christ will appear visibly at the beginning of the one thousand-year period; hence they are called Premillennialists. Others claim that Christ will come after the millennium, hence they are called Postmillennialists. The great majority belong to the first class. Christians who reject all physical interpretations of the second advent are called Amillennialists.

It will be helpful to present a brief outline of the reasons why millennialists teach as they do. They believe:

1. All predictions about the Messiah's kingdom must be literally fulfilled.
2. There is a difference between God's kingdom (the holy Christian church) and Christ's kingdom, His reign in the millennium.
3. Israel is to become a light to the Gentiles, something that cannot happen until Israel is converted.
4. In the millennium Christ will compel all mankind to acknowledge His lordship.

5. The millennium will be a visible, earthly kingdom of universal blessings.

Millennialists have established a sequence of main events for the millennium:

1. Christ will come to earth invisibly to resurrect the deceased believers and transfigure the living believers so that they may be removed or "raptured" from this earth during the "great tribulation."
2. The great tribulation will last seven years. During this time the Antichrist will be revealed and the Jewish people will be converted to Christ.
3. Now Christ will establish His kingdom and judge all nations on the basis of their treatment of the Jews.
4. Christ will reign for a thousand years. Toward the end of this period Satan will be set free for a short time before his ultimate destruction.
5. At the end of the millennium there will be a "second resurrection" followed by a final judgment, in which hell and death will be totally destroyed and a new heaven and a new earth will come into being (Mayer, pp. 427—431, where there are many further details).

Historically, the majority of Christians have rejected chiliasm because they could find no basis for its teachings in the Bible. They believed that the prophecies about the splendor of Christ's kingdom must be interpreted spiritually as references to the glory of the New Testament church. Specifically, these Christians believe that the Bible speaks of only one visible return of Christ to this earth, namely on the Last Day for the final judgment. They find no support in Scripture for a distinction between God's kingdom and Christ's kingdom. Nor do they see any Scriptural proof for the claim that the Jewish nation as such (all the descendants of Abraham "after the flesh") will be converted to Christ *en masse.* Finally, those opposed to millennial teachings believe that emphasis on a millennial kingdom of earthly blessings and glories turns the Christian's hope away from eternal life in heaven to some earthly paradise.

A peculiar form of chiliasm is called dispensationalism, since it holds that God deals with mankind in history in a variety of different ways or "dispensations." Taking the week of creation described in Genesis 1 as its starting point, dispensationalism teaches that all of history must be divided into seven distinct periods. As God performed a different creative work on each of the first six days and rested on the seventh day, so God has a new way of dealing with people during six dispensations, climaxing in the seventh era, the millennium. Individual dispensationalists divide history differently, but most agree that Old Testament history comprises five dispensations and that the New Testament age is the sixth. Dispensationalism centers on the history and destiny of the Jewish people to such an extent that the New Testament church is called a "parenthesis church," a temporary interruption of God's basic activity.

In the view of Christians who oppose this scheme, there is no Biblical basis for the claim that God deals with mankind in a number of different ways, since the Gospel of God's mercy is the same throughout history. There is no foundation in Scripture for making Israel the center of world history, rather than the work of Christ and the New Testament church. Nor is there any warrant for making the Sermon on the Mount, rather than the Gospel, the definitive message of God to man.

The Seventh-Day Adventists

As the name suggests, this church has two main emphases in its teaching: Observance of the seventh day, or Sabbath, and the second coming, or advent, of Christ. Early in the 19th century William Miller, a farmer who became a Baptist preacher, concluded from his study of the Bible that Christ's advent and the beginning of the millennium could be precisely dated. This involved the interpretation of numbers and designations of time mentioned in the Bible, such as 3, 7, 1000, day, week, month, year. Starting with Daniel 8:13, 14, which says that the sanctuary, or temple, would be desecrated for 2300 days, Miller reasoned that each "day" represented a year. Therefore at the end of 2300 years the desecration of the temple would cease and a new, good time, namely the millennium, would begin. Miller believed that the year 457 B.C., when the command to rebuild Jerusalem was given, was the point of departure. 2300 - 457 = 1843 A.D. Christ's advent to begin the millennium was, therefore, scheduled to occur some time during that year. When nothing unusual happened, it was claimed that there had been a slight error in calculation and that Christ would appear visibly on October 22, 1844. When this, too, ended in disappointment, most of Miller's followers deserted him and returned to their own churches.

However, another explanation of Miller's apparent failure was proposed, namely, that his dates were correct but his description of what was to happen then was mistaken. This was the claim of a Mrs. Ellen G. White who, together with her husband and others, had been a strong supporter of Miller. Mrs. White alleged that she had visions and received prophetic messages direct from God. In one of her visions she claimed to have seen a narrow path leading to the heavenly Jerusalem, with none but Adventists walking on it. Another vision gave Mrs. White an understanding of the message of the three angels mentioned in Revelation 14:6 ff. William Miller had, in fact, been correct about 1843-44, but the event took place in heaven. God's hour of judgment had come, the wicked Babylon had fallen when Adventists left the regular denominations, and, thirdly, there was a warning against worshiping the beast, the Antichrist, who compelled Christians to observe Sunday in place of the Sabbath. Thus Mrs. White combined Miller's chiliasm with seventh-day observance. Seventh-Day Adventists regard Mrs. White's writings as "inspired counsel from the Lord."

In addition to the Sabbath law, Adventists believe that many other Old Testament precepts, such as the tithe and laws pertaining to diet, are still in force for Christians.

Adventists do not share the general Christian belief in the immortality of the soul. A leading Seventh-Day Adventist author writes that

they hold that life comes only from Christ, the source of life. No one, they assert, can have eternal life apart from Christ. Man by himself is mortal, subject to death. Only Christ can make him immortal. And immortality, says the Bible, will not be conferred until the resurrection at the second coming of Christ in glory.

Seventh-day Adventists hold that the ancient supposition that people go to heaven or hell immediately upon death is an infiltration of pagan mythology into Christian theology. Bible teaching on this subject, they claim, is as clear as day—that *the dead are asleep until the glorious return of Jesus Christ as King of Kings and Lord of Lords.* Then, but not until then, will final rewards and punishments be meted out (Arthur S. Maxwell, "What Is a Seventh-day Adventist?" in Rosten, pp. 184 f., emphases added).

This teaching is called psychopannychism, or soul sleep.

Of the nearly one million members throughout the world, some 300,000 are in the United States.

Chapter 9

The Cults

In his book on the denominations the Roman Catholic William J. Whalen introduces his section on the cults by saying that

> we find a variety of religious bodies commonly identified as Christian although they cannot make the remotest claim to the title. Some of these groups deny the most fundamental Christian beliefs such as the divinity of Christ, the existence of evil, the trinity, original sin, and the redemption, but they enjoy the prestige which accrues to a Christian church in a professedly Christian nation.
>
> . . . .
>
> ... we will discuss a number of cults which we must classify as "Christians by courtesy." A careful examination of their tenets will disclose no warrant for extending to them the title "Christian" even though the cultists themselves may appropriate the name (William J. Whalen, *Separated Brethren*, Milwaukee: The Bruce Publishing Company, 1961, pp. 147 f.).

The word "cult" is often used to refer to religious groups that have come into being and are maintained by commitment to teachings that have little or nothing in common with the historic Christian faith, even though they may use Christian terminology and have a place for Jesus in their system and may regard themselves as Christian. Yet frequently they stand in isolation from historic Christian churches and even in vigorous opposition to them.

It will be useful at this point to review what is basic to Biblical Christianity. Bearing in mind what Christians believe will be helpful in determining whether the claims advanced by a religious group conform to what is Christian. The ancient ecumenical creeds present the most concise summary of the Christian faith. This includes belief in the triune God, Father, Son, and Holy Spirit, as the only true God. Luther: "These articles of the Creed, therefore, divide and distinguish us Christians from all other people on earth" (Large Catechism,

Creed, 66, Tappert, p.419), that is to say, anyone who denies the triune God is not a Christian. To be Christian means to acknowledge the reality of sin and evil in every human being and his total inability to save himself from God's judgment. To be Christian means to believe that God has provided for the salvation of all sinners through His eternal Son, Jesus Christ, by His suffering, death, and resurrection, and that He is the only Savior. To be Christian includes faith in the work of the Holy Spirit to bring people to trust in God and to lead sanctified lives. To be Christian involves believing in the holy Christian church as the community of believers where the Gospel in Word and Sacrament is in use. To be Christian means to look for the return of Christ on the last day for His final judgment, with the gift of eternal life for all believers and eternal death for all who spurned God's offer of salvation through Jesus Christ. Christians believe that the Bible is the Word of God and therefore the only source of Christian teaching.

These are all elements of what it means to be Christian. This does not mean, however, that unless a person grasps and expresses these truths perfectly he is not a Christian. Nor does a person's failure to live up to the full implications of the Christian faith mean that he has forfeited his Christianity. If that were the case, no one could be a Christian, for, as Luther points out, "we daily sin much and indeed deserve nothing but punishment" (Small Catechism, 5th Petition), and all Christians must live by the daily forgiveness of sins. Furthermore, not all items included in the Christian religion are on the same level of importance. Reduced to the irreducible minimum, whether a person is a Christian or not is determined by that person's relationship "to the office and work of Jesus Christ, or to our redemption" (Smalcald Articles, Tappert, p. 292). Faith in Jesus Christ makes one a Christian.

> The first and chief article is this, that Jesus Christ, our God and Lord, "was put to death for our trespasses and raised again for our justification" (Rom. 4:25). He alone is the "the Lamb of God, who takes away the sin of the world" (John 1:29). "God has laid upon him the iniquities of us all" (Isaiah 53:6). Moreover, "all have sinned," and "they are justified by his grace as a gift, through the redemption which is in Christ Jesus, by his blood" (Rom. 3:23-25).
>
> . . . .
>
> Nothing in this article can be given up or compromised (ibid.).

But where there is explicit denial of basic Christian truth, it is fair to raise the question whether individuals or groups espousing these denials are properly to be called Christian. Such a judgment must, of course, be restricted to what is explicitly taught or denied. It is quite possible that individual members of sub-Christian or non-Christian cults are Christians in spite of their association, however weak and fragmentary their understanding and belief may be. Against the backdrop of these considerations we proceed to look at a few of these cults.

A. Jehovah's Witnesses

This religious group is little more than 100 years old (1872). The founder was Charles T. Russell, who took over some of the ideas of the Adventists, such as date-setting, the annihilation of the wicked, and the nearness of Christ's return and developed them further. He was a dispensationalist, but divided history into three separate areas instead of the usual seven. Each period is said to offer man the chance to earn the right to live forever, if he will obey God's law. The angels are said to have been in charge of the first dispensation which ended with the Flood. During the time of the second "world" Satan was in control until 1914, when he was expelled from heaven. That year was to mark the beginning of the third "world," the perfect golden age. Russell was succeeded by Joseph F. Rutherford, 1916-1942, followed by Nathan H. Knorr. Earlier in their history the followers were known as Russellites, Millennial Dawnists, or International Bible Students. Since 1931 they bear the name Jehovah's Witnesses.

Their headquarters are in Brooklyn, New York, with the official title, The Watchtower Bible and Tract Society of New York, Inc. Local groups do not regard themselves as churches but as congregations, and their meeting places are called "kingdom halls." The movement promotes itself by means of a vigorous, highly developed and organized missionary effort and system of indoctrination which a former long-time member labeled "seven steps of brain-washing" (W. J. Schnell, *Thirty Years a Watchtower Slave, The Confessions of a Converted Jehovah's Witness*, Grand Rapids: Baker Book House, 1956, pp. 131 ff.). Every member is considered a minister or "publisher," and all of them are expected to devote considerable time to missionary work. The central theory of this cult may be summarized as follows:

Jehovah created this world to be the everlasting home of man on condition that man prove his obedience to Jehovah. Lucifer,

67

the lord of the visible world, however, became disobedient and challenged Jehovah to put a creature on this earth who would not blaspheme and reproach Him. Thereupon Jehovah created man and gave Lucifer, or Satan, permission to do everything in his power to tempt man to blaspheme Jehovah, so that it would become evident that man can keep the laws of Jehovah's theocracy. Of course, at the present time Satan is still ruling the world, and only comparatively few are able to recognize the claims of the Lord Jehovah. But Satan's dominion will soon be destroyed, and God's theocracy will be established. Mankind will be obedient. This world will be under Jehovah's everlasting kingdom. God's original purpose in creating the world will be realized. Jehovah's Witnesses believe that they have been raised to announce the early establishment of God's theocracy (Mayer, p. 466).

The Witnesses affirm that the only true God is Jehovah. This name is said to be derived from the most sacred title given to God in the Old Testament, a word of four consonants JHWH. It was not pronounced by the Israelites, but whenever it occurred, they substituted the name Adonai, the Hebrew word for "my Lord." Greek translations of the Old Testament use the word *Kyrios*, Lord, for JHWH, also in the Greek New Testament, a practice followed by most English translations. Many of the JHWH passages of the Old Testament are quoted in the New Testament and applied directly to the Lord Jesus Christ. Although they claim to worship none but the true God Jehovah, Witnesses refer to the Trinity as "that notorious pagan doctrine" (Van Baalen, p. 240).

Rutherford, the second leader of the cult, declared:

The doctrine of the "trinity" finds no support whatsoever in the Bible, but on the contrary, the Bible proves beyond all doubt that it is the Devil's doctrine, fraudulently imposed upon men to destroy their faith in Jehovah God and His gracious provision for the redemption and regeneration of the human race. Therefore it definitely appears that the doctrine of the so-called "holy trinity" is another of Satan's lies (cited in Mayer, p. 469).

Jehovah's Witnesses teach that in Satan's efforts to keep people from obeying Jehovah he is assisted by three allies, namely, the churches, big business, and governments. In the words of Rutherford

In these latter times the three elements, under the supervision of the Devil, have united in forming the most subtle and wicked world power of all time (Mayer, p. 471).

Members have, therefore, been outspoken in their opposition to the church, and they refuse to salute the flag or participate in any wars waged by the government.

Witnesses affirm that Jesus was not the Son of God, coequal with the Father, but a creature, only a man, and they view His work of atonement as incomplete, to be supplemented by man's returning to God through his own free will. Man, they say, does not have a soul; he is a soul, and death means total annihilation.

Mankind is divided into four separate groups:

1. The 144,000, also called the "great mystery class," or the "bride of Christ." They are the "body of Christ" and by their obedience to Jehovah they have earned the right to live forever.

2. The Old Testament believers. These cannot have immortality because they lived before Jesus accomplished His task. But they will dwell on earth in the visible part of God's kingdom. Rutherford even had a large structure erected in San Diego, California, that was to be the residence of returning Old Testament saints such as Abraham, David, and others. The place was called *Beth Sarim* (House of Princes). It was sold in 1948.

3. The Jonadab class, also known as the "multitude," "other sheep," or the "people of good will." This group is said to consist of all the people who were friendly to Jehovah's Witnesses.

4. The people who will be given the opportunity to prove their loyalty to Jehovah in the kingdom to come. These are the ones who failed to obey Jehovah when they lived on earth because they were ignorant of His real nature. They will be raised in the millennium and given another chance.

Of the worldwide total of a million and a quarter active adherents about one third of a million are in the United States.

B. The Church of Jesus Christ of Latter-Day Saints (Mormons)

If Jehovah's Witnesses may be said to be of American origin, this applies with even greater force to the Mormons. The claims made in connection with their movement are inseparably linked with the Western hemisphere, the "new world." Not only was the founder of this religion an American, but important features of the system have to do with events that are said to have taken place first in South America and then in North America.

Mormonism may be evaluated from more than one perspective. Regarded strictly as an experiment in communal agriculture and industry with great social implications, it offers much of a positive nature. Settling in Utah, when it was still a part of Mexico, many thousands of Mormons who had made the long trek across the plains established a powerful community with far-reaching impact on the surrounding Western states. They have evinced a strong concern for the physical well-being of all their members, so that none need to go hungry or look for help from the government or other sources. Mormons place strong emphasis on the solidarity and welfare of the family. In order to provide for all family and social as well as religious needs, they expect all their members to contribute at least ten percent of all their money and goods to the church. They display an unmatched zeal for the spread of their religious system and demand the free service of their members to promote it throughout the world.

Our interest, however, is chiefly theological. What are the teachings of Mormonism and how do they compare with traditional Christianity?

It all started with Joseph Smith, a farmer's boy near Palmyra, New York. He was given to dreaming and serious reflection on the religious scene in his neighborhood. He was deeply upset by the differences among the denominations. While he wondered about which church he should join, he claimed that he had a vision of two angels, or transfigured persons, who told him not to join any existing church, since they had all become untrue and the Gospel was lost. A few years later the angel Moroni appeared to him and commissioned him to translate a number of golden plates reputedly hidden in the Hill Cumorah, near Palmyra. The plates were allegedly written in "Reformed Egyptian," and Smith was provided with mysterious spectacles called Urim and Thummim, which enabled this uneducated lad and a few associates to translate the golden plates. Thus *The Book of Mormon* came into being, according to Smith's own account. On April 6, 1830, Smith, together with five others, chief among them Sydney Rigdon, organized the Church of Jesus Christ of Latter-Day Saints. Smith claimed special revelations and was regarded by his followers as an inspired prophet, just like the Biblical prophets of old.

During the next few years the group moved around, first to

Kirtland, Ohio, then to Independence, Missouri, and then to Nauvoo, Illinois, on the Mississippi River. Here they established a thriving community, at one time the largest city in Illinois. Smith even ran for president of the United States. However, because of strange teachings, including the promotion of polygamy, the hostility of other people was aroused, and Joseph Smith and his brother Hyrum were murdered by a mob. It was then that a young and gifted follower of Smith, Brigham Young, assumed control of the movement and guided the entire community to Salt Lake City, Utah. A splinter group, claiming that a descendant of Smith must be in charge and repudiating some of Young's teachings, settled in Independence, Missouri, and called themselves the Reorganized Church of Jesus Christ of Latter-Day Saints. When Utah Territory applied for statehood, the United States government would not grant it unless the Mormons abrogated the practice of polygamy. Thereupon Wilford Woodruff, the president of the church, decreed on October 6, 1890: "My advice to the Latter-Day Saints is to refrain from contracting marriages forbidden by law of the land" *(Doctrines and Covenants*, Mayer, p. 461, n. 28).

The doctrinal system of Mormonism is quite complicated and appears to include elements drawn from a variety of sources. Yet there are some basic premises:

First, the eternal existence of a living personal God and the pre-existence and eternal duration of mankind as His literal offspring; and, second, the placing of man upon the earth as an embodied spirit to undergo the experiences of an intermediate probation (Mayer, p.455).

Throughout its history the Christian church has looked to the Holy Scriptures as the authoritative source for its teachings. Mormons also regard the Bible as God's Word, especially for the "old world," for the believers of ancient times. But in addition, there is *The Book of Mormon* for the Western world and for the more recent believers, hence the "latter-day saints." Mormons also believe in God's continued revelations to Smith and other leaders after him, and these are even more important than the Bible and the Book of Mormon. These revelations are said to be recorded in *The Pearl of Great Price* and in *Doctrines and Covenants.*

According to *The Book of Mormon,* many people of Asia crossed the ocean and settled in South America thousands of years before Christ. By about 600 B.C. they had died out but left behind a record of their history on 24 golden plates, which were found by Moroni later.

There was said to have been another emigration from Jerusalem to America, notably a certain Lehi and his family. The descendants of his son, Nephi, were godly and produced a very high culture. Jesus is supposed to have appeared to the Nephites after His ascension and established His church. The descendants of Laman, another son of Lehi, were evil and warred against the Nephites. The Lamanites were punished by being made dark-skinned and were the ancestors of the Indians. Around 400 A.D. the last survivor of the Nephites, the angel Moroni, son of Mormon, managed to carry the golden plates from South America to upstate New York and buried them in the Hill Cumorah, where Joseph Smith claimed to have found them.

Many scholars regard as conclusive the evidence that *The Book of Mormon* was put together by Joseph Smith and Sidney Rigdon on the basis of an unpublished novel by Solomon Spaulding, a Presbyterian clergyman. The novel was titled *The Manuscript Found*, and it purports to relate the origin of the American Indians. (Further details in J. K. Van Baalen, pp. 151 f.; Mayer, pp. 456 f.)

Mormons believe in a plurality of gods. The Father and the Son are pictured as physical beings, while the Holy Spirit is called a "personage of spirit." It is taught that there is an eternal progression among gods as well as men, according to the Mormon axiom: "As man is, God once was; as God is, man may be."

Regarding man it is said that "man himself has existed from the premortal past and will continue, with his individual identity, into the endless eternal future" (Richard L. Evans, "What Is a Mormon"? in Rosten, p. 135). Man must pass through three periods of probation: preexistence, incarnation, and after death. Before incarnation man is a soul without a body and must rely upon the union of men and women on earth to be provided with a body. Marriage and family therefore play a central role in Mormonism. According to Evans, the

> Mormon believes that there can be no heaven for him without his family, and if he fully conforms to the teachings of his Church, he enters into a marriage covenant that lasts not only until "death do us part" but continues "for time and eternity" (Rosten p. 137).

However, only marriages performed in secret Mormon temple rites share in this privilege and are called celestial marriages.

When Mormons speak of Jesus Christ as the Savior, their meaning seems to be that His work of atonement consisted in His rising to immortality and thus making it possible for man to work out his own salvation after death. For those who did not achieve it during this life there is said to be another chance after death.

Mormonism claims well over two million members.

C. Christian Science

Christian Science is the name given by its founder, Mary Baker Eddy, to the solutions she discovered in her search for physical and mental well-being. Born in Bow, New Hampshire, the daughter of a devout farmer, Mary Baker experienced considerable illness and nervous affliction during her childhood and youth. In her adult years she manifested a strong and dominating will. She was married three times, first to George Washington Glover, a contractor, who died within the year. They had a son, who was born after Glover's death. Mary's second marriage was to Dr. Daniel Patterson, a dentist, from whom she was divorced after a few years. At age 56 she married Asa Gilbert Eddy, a sewing machine agent, who selflessly devoted himself to his wife's interests, until he died of heart disease. Although this was attested as the cause of death by physicians who had performed an autopsy, Mrs. Eddy believed that her husband had been "poisoned by arsenic mentally administered."

Frequent attacks of illness and pain drove Mrs. Eddy to the use of morphine and to further search for relief. In 1862 she discovered a certain Phineas Parkhurst Quimby, of Portland, Maine, who practiced healing by means of mesmerism, or hypnotism, or "mental electricity." During a stay of several weeks in Portland Mrs. Eddy was cured of her nervous condition through Quimby's treatments, and she eagerly read his manuscripts and absorbed his ideas of healing. Later she spent an even longer period of time under his guidance. The influence of Quimby's ideas on Mrs. Eddy's writings is clearly traceable. For her book, *Science and Health with Key to the Scriptures*, first published in 1875, Mrs. Eddy later made this claim:

> I should blush to write a Science and Health with Key to the Scriptures as I have, were it of human origin, and I, apart from God, its author; but as I was only a scribe echoing the harmonies of heaven in divine metaphysics, I cannot be super-modest in my estimate of the Christian Science textbook *(Christian Science Journal*, January 1901, cited by George W. Wittmer, *Christian Science in the Light of the Bible*. St. Louis: Concordia, 1949, p. 27).

In 1879 Mrs. Eddy organized the Church of Christ (Scientist) at Boston. Two years later she founded the Massachusetts Metaphysical College. During the next decade she taught some 4,000 students a 12-lesson course in healing for $300 each. At the time of her death she left an estate of around $3,000,000. Her declining years were spent in increasing seclusion from the outside world, until she died in 1910 at the age of 89 years.

The Key to the Scriptures appended to her book, *Science and Health*, offers a glossary of Biblical terms as reinterpreted by Mrs. Eddy, designed to give metaphysical, or "spiritual," meaning to them. Here are some of her definitions:

Creator. Spirit; Mind, intelligence; the animating divine Principle of all that is real and good, self-existent Life, Truth, and Love; the opposite of matter and evil, which have no Principle.

Death. An illusion, the lie of life in matter; matter has no life, hence it has no real existence. Mind is immortal.

God. The great I AM; Principle; Mind; Soul; Spirit; Life; Truth; Love.

Jesus. The highest human corporeal concept of the divine idea, rebuking and destroying error and bringing to light man's immortality.

Man. The compound idea of infinite Spirit.

Matter. Mythology; mortality; another name for mortal mind; illusion; intelligence, substance, and life in non-intelligence and mortality; sensation in the sensationless; mind orignating in matter; that of which immortal Mind takes no cognizance; that which mortal mind sees, feels, hears, tastes, and smells only in belief.

Mortal Mind. Nothing claiming to be something, for Mind is immortal; error creating other errors; sensation is in matter, which is sensationless.

Mother. God; divine and eternal Principle; Life, Truth, and Love *(Science and Health*, pp. 479-99).

Christian Science worship services consist of music, Bible readings, prayers, and a "lesson-sermon" composed of passages from the Bible and *Science and Health*. Often there are spontaneous testimonials of healing by members.

Christian Science makes much use of Biblical terms, including the divine names, God Father, Son, Holy Spirit. Nevertheless, it is very difficult to find traditional Christian teaching expressed in the way these terms are being defined and used. Mrs. Eddy expressed the core of her message in four "self-evident" and "mathematically proved" propositions said to be reversible, that is, capable of being read and making sense both forward and backward:

1. God is all-in-all.
2. God is good. God is Mind.
3. God, Spirit, being all, nothing is matter.
4. Life, God, omnipotent Good, deny death, evil, sins, disease *(Science and Health,* pp. 475 f.).

To Mrs. Eddy the only reality is divine Mind. All matter is unreal. All disease, evil, and death is nonexistent, having reality only in man's failure to overcome the thought of their nonexistence. To the degree that people arrive at the knowledge that evil and pain do not exist, they have been fully "healed" and made perfect. Sin, too, is regarded as unreal, and therefore there need be and can be no deliverance from sin. Even the death of Jesus was unreal. Here, then, there appears to be a "'religion' which teaches that there is nothing to be saved from, and no one to be saved from, and no one to be saved" (Van Baalen, p. 107). Another offers this summary of Christian Science: "An abstract idea (Christ or Truth) has freed the error of mortal minds (the human body) from another error of mortal mind (sin) by a third error of mortal mind (the death of Jesus)" (Mayer, p. 542).

Since local branches of Christian Science are forbidden to publish membership statistics, it is not possible to give an accurate figure. Some estimates place the number of followers as high as 500,000 predominantly among the economic, social, and cultural upper classes. Recently, however, there is strong evidence of a very serious decline in membership.

*   *   *

There are literally hundreds of other groups and organizations in America that claim some religious orientation in dealing with the important questions of man's origins, condition, and destiny, of how to meet human needs for coping with the great issues of life and death. It is impossible to deal with them all, nor is that necessary. The churches and religious groups discussed in these pages account for well above 90 percent of all people in the United States claiming membership in any church. Since our survey is limited to bodies aligned in name or substance with Christianity, there is no treatment of Judaism, Islam, or any other non-Christian religion. Furthermore, many groups are extremely small, or bizarre, or transitory, or minor variations of older and larger theological traditions, that we may dispense with their individual analyses. Any mature Christian with an understanding of the basics of the Christian faith should be in a position to evaluate the claims of any system that offers itself for consideration and acceptance.

Chapter 10

Concluding Reflections

A survey of the religious scene in America can be a bewildering experience. Hundreds of religious groups competing for the devotion and support of the people, claiming to draw their ideas from the same source, the Bible, yet in serious disagreement with each other, offering contradictory solutions to human problems—this situation surely gives rise to some questions. How do denominations come into being? Why are there such profound differences? What lessons may be learned from this state of affairs? How should we act toward Christians of another church or adherents of another religion?

Jan Karel Van Baalen observes:

> More and more I have come to the conclusion that we can learn from cultists, not only noting what not to believe, but also bearing in mind that "the cults are the unpaid bills of the church" *(The Chaos of Cults*, p. 14).

> At the same time, a study of the cults may well humble us because most of them are the result of an insufficient emphasis by Christians upon some valuable point of Biblical teaching: the boast that we preach "the full counsel of God" is all too often vain, untrue, and the fruit of a narrowed view which is due to a refusal to look beyond one's own small group (ibid., p.19).

Such reflections ought to lead us to address searching questions to ourselves regarding our own church: Why did this or that splinter group arise? Was it because we failed people? If so, where and how? Are there legitimate spiritual needs that we have failed to meet? Although what we teach is Biblical, did we omit anything that we should have said and done? Are there accents in our theology that have been forgotten? What should we do to make our church not only doctrinally sound but sensitive and responsive to all proper human needs?

No attempt will be made to answer all of these questions. The important thing is that we are alert to them and keep them before us as we try to do justice to our relationships with others, without sacrificing or compromising our own religious convictions.

Why, then, do we have so many divergent denominations? Certainly a common human perversity accounts for some of the problems. People have always, in the past and down to the present, failed to take God's Word on God's terms, choosing rather to bring their own prejudices and biases to the Scriptures and forcing them to say what they themselves wanted. Geographical, historical, and political factors may have played a role in molding certain groups in a specific way. The personal problems of certain individuals and the dominating personalities of some religious leaders may have contributed to a movement's affirmations. There have been personality cults, where adherents blindly followed the dictates of charismatic leaders. Yet these matters cannot account altogether for the Christian varieties that confront us.

Throughout the church's history people have endeavored to formulate their teaching by way of reaction to what they regarded as overstatements or one-sided formulations. These reactions, in turn, often went too far, and these again evoked extreme responses, like the course of a pendulum, swinging from one extreme to the other. In the ancient church one school of theology, centering in Alexandria, stressed the divine side of our Lord's nature to such an extent that His true humanity appeared to receive less than its due. Another school of theology, centered in Antioch, Syria, focused on Christ's human side and gave less than adequate consideration to His deity and did not know how to formulate the relation of both to each other in the one person, Jesus Christ. Or, while theologians concentrated on the person of the Redeemer, they failed to do justice to His saving work. After generations of controversy, the Council of Chalcedon, in 451, proceeded to combine all of these accents in one meaningful definition.

Lutherans have always been identified as people who stressed justification by faith. In fact, they complained that this teaching is labeled a Lutheran peculiarity. "This blessed doctrine, the precious holy Gospel, they call Lutheran" (Apology of the Augsburg Confession XV, 42, German paraphrase; *Concordia Triglotta*, p. 327). While all Christians believe in justification by faith, many felt that Lutherans often spoke of it in a one-sided way, as an end in itself, without pointing up its inseparable connection with sanctification, the new, holy life. By way of reaction, many put the primary accent on sanctification in a way that seemed to Lutherans a slighting of justification. Thus John Wesley understood Luther:

78

Who wrote more ably on Justification by Faith alone than Martin Luther, and who was more ignorant of the doctrine of Sanctification or more confused in his conception of it? On the other hand, how many writers of the Roman Church . . . have written strongly and scripturally on Sanctification, who, nevertheless, were entirely unacquainted with the doctrine of justification . . . (Mayer, p. 292, n. 35).

Some have thought of God as utterly transcendent, so far removed from the affairs of this world that He has no interest in, or contact with, it. Therefore the world was conceived as closed, with no divine intervention from outside. In reaction, many have gone to the other extreme and insisted that far from being distant, God was very near, in fact, already present within every person. It is not difficult to see what consequences such approaches to God will have for the teaching about the Word and the sacraments.

Some have minimized or rejected outright all concepts dealing with the heareafter, heaven and hell, eternal life and eternal damnation. There is no other world after this one, they maintained. Whatever bliss or bane, heaven or hell there may be, is to be experienced in this life, here and now. Eschatology is not something for the future, but it is being realized in the present. In reaction, many have placed the last things into the center of their faith to the detriment of other Biblical teaching.

Some have held views of the church with strong emphasis on the corporate concept that seemed to others to minimize the importance of the individual. The reaction was to place the individual into the center to the detriment of the body. Some teachings about the ministry have insisted that the validity and effectiveness of official acts depended upon specific forms of church government, of grades of the clergy, and of receiving ordination and authorization from such as could trace their ordination back to the apostles. In reaction, others have rejected all elements of church government and official authorization and made every individual sovereign, rendering any kind of orderly procedure impossible.

Some have laid great stress on prescribed forms of worship, on vestments, on appointments for the house of worship. Any deviation from the liturgical prescriptions were regarded by many as serious infractions. Many others saw in such emphases a cold formalism, an insistence upon form for form's sake that appeared to stifle all personal initiative and individual expression. People were repelled by the rigid rule of rubrics and in reaction scuttled all formally structured worship, so that every individual might have free rein to give vent to the feelings of his heart. Corporate, objective forms were supplanted by subjective "heart religion," as Pietism reacted to formal orthodoxy in Lutheran Germany, and Methodism rose in protest against Anglican formalism.

It has been suggested that while none of the great historic Christian churches denies any of the properties ascribed to God in the Scriptures, none of them emphasizes the same property as the others. This approach to the doctrine of God is said to influence the whole conception of God, and this, in turn, influences other points of doctrine (Wilhelm Walther, *Lehrbuch der Symbolik.* "Die Eigentümlichkeiten der vier christlichen Hauptkirchen." Leipzig: A. Deichertsche Verlagsbuchhandlung, 1924, p. 9).

Pursuing this suggestion, we might say that Eastern Orthodoxy stressed God's goodness in terms of a benevolent attitude that minimized the seriousness of sin. Roman Catholicism, it could be argued, placed God's punitive and rewarding justice into the center, resulting in a teaching of work-righteousness. A case could be made for tracing the heavy legalism often manifested in Calvinism back to its accent on God's absolute sovereignty. Some might find the cause of relatively little activism among Lutherans in their predominant emphasis on God's grace. This insight is indeed thought-provoking, but it would be an oversimplification and tend to unfair judgments to consider it in isolation from other factors.

Other manifestations of one-sidedness would be the tendency to focus on one person of the Holy Trinity to the neglect of the others. An unbalanced emphasis on the "fatherhood of God" has led to a disparagement of the work of Jesus Christ and the Holy Spirit. A certain kind of concentration on Jesus has resulted in what has been called "Jesus mania" or "Jesus-Unitarianism." Many people have felt that the teaching of mainline churches has neglected the activity of the Holy Spirit and have therefore developed a "Spirit" theology in a one-sided way.

It would seem that there is an infinite variety of possibilities of failing to proclaim "the whole counsel of God." Ultimately, it comes down to the way people read, understand, and teach the content of the Bible and apply its teaching to life. It is of extreme importance not only to see what the words of Scripture say but also to discover what they mean—what God is communicating to mankind through His Word. In an approach to the writing of any author it is of paramount importance to hear him out on his terms in order to do justice to his message and purpose. It is even more crucial to follow this course in approaching the Word of God. We are dealing with the proper exegesis, or interpretation, of the Scriptures, on the basis of the proper principles of interpretation, or, to use the technical term, hermeneutics (derived from the Greek word meaning "interpret"). It is not enough to say, "It's in the Bible" to insure the correctness of one's teaching. Many extreme and bizarre religious notions are being promoted on the plea that their source is the Bible.

The collection of documents constituting the Christian Scriptures covers some 1,500 or more years of writing by a great variety of authors, writing in different lands, in different languages, in different degrees of ability and education and literary style, addressed to many different kinds of people under a host of divergent circumstances. These writings contain much history, centering in one particular nation in the near East, the people of Israel, and involving the nations surrounding the Mediterranean Sea to the extent their actions impinged on Israel. The books of the Bible have much to say about outstanding individuals. Much insight is given into a variety of contemporary social customs. Amid all this diversity of content, there is an ever present danger of getting lost in side issues and missing the central point.

The question is not whether the content of the Bible is "true" and "reliable." Of course it is. Nor is the issue whether some parts of the Bible are Word of God and some, word of man. In a very real sense, all of it is both, since God chose to convey His address to mankind through human tongues and pens, speaking the common human language. Yet all of it is the Word of God. If so, it cannot be that some of it is important and some of it is not. It's all important. Yet there are levels and degrees of importance.

Thus, although the Bible teems with historical facts, it is not a textbook on ancient history. Though the lives and careers of a number of great human beings are detailed, the Bible is not a collection of biographical sketches. Though a number of the documents offer a great deal of information about Jesus Christ, their purpose is not to offer "lives" of Jesus. Although there are many literary forms in the Bible and although much of the content ranks with the most glorious products of human letters, the Bible was not given to be "read as living literature." Although the pages of Scripture are replete with references to certain numbers that occur again and again, like 3, 7, 12, or multiples of these, the Bible is not written in a secret numerical code for which one must find a key. Although the Bible records scores of laws and precepts, it is not a rule book with automatic application. Hence there can be no quantitative concern, such as, how many writings belong into the Bible, or how much I have to know, or how much I must do.

Since we affirm that the Bible is God's Word, the single overriding question must be: What is God up to? That, and that alone, can be the key to the Scriptures and their correct understanding. The answer to the big question can only be derived from the Word. Once that has been determined, it must provide the perspective for the interpretation of the rest.

God's disclosure of His works and His plans came to man in a gradual unfolding until it reached its climax.

> In many and various ways God spoke of old to our fathers by the prophets; but in these last days He has spoken to us by a Son, whom He appointed the heir of all things, through whom also He created the world. He reflects the glory of God and bears the very stamp of His nature, upholding the universe by His word of power. When He had made purification for sins, He sat down at the right hand of the Majesty on high (Hebrews 1:1-3).

As the climax of His message to mankind, God revealed Himself in person, in His only Son. "No one has ever seen God; the only Son, who is in the bosom of the Father, He has made Him known" (John 1:18). What is God up to? What does He have in mind for us? "The Word became flesh and dwelt among us, full of grace and truth" (John 1:14). Jesus Christ, God's Son, is God's way of reconciling the world to Himself. This is the center of the Scriptures, this is the sum and purpose of God's revelation. Jesus did not come to impose additional laws on people who were already under God's judgment because of their failure to keep His commandments, but to redeem them from the curse of the Law. God's ultimate Word to mankind, therefore, is a Person. Our proper response must be a person-to-person relationship, a response of trust and love and obedience. This provides the proper perspective for studying the Bible.

And that is also the perspective from which we look at the many Christian varieties and attempt to evaluate them. We are not asked to ignore, let alone approve, any clear departure from God's truth. Error can never be a matter of indifference. However, we should be quite certain that the differences between us and other people are really a question of right and wrong, and not just different ways of saying the same thing, just as the same truth may be expressed by a variety of Biblical terms and images. We must be equally careful not to exaggerate the points of difference. Not everything is on the same level of importance. Remembering the ultimate content and purpose of God's address to mankind, the decisive question is: "What do you think of the Christ?" (Matthew 22:42). Where the Gospel of the grace of God in Christ is proclaimed, there is "the church's one foundation" (f. 1 Corinthians 3:11), that is,

> the true knowledge of Christ and faith. Of course, there are also many weak people in it who build on this foundation perishing structures of stubble, that is, unprofitable opinions. But because they do not overthrow the foundation, these are forgiven them or even corrected (Apology, Augsburg Confession, VII, 20; Tappert, pp. 171 f.).

We are living in an age of great mobility and instant communication. It may have been possible in the past for many people to live out their entire lives in isolation from people of differing religious views. This is no longer possible today. This is also the era of the so-called ecumenical movement. Christian churches of various denominations have worldwide federations, such as the Roman Catholic Church, the Eastern Orthodox churches, the Anglican Communion, the Lutheran World Federation, the World Alliance of Reformed Churches Holding the Presbyterian Order, and others. In addition, most of the major church bodies are associated in the World Council of Churches, where, especially in the Faith and Order section, there is much joint theological study and dialog. A new spirit of willingness on the part of Christians to engage Christians of other denominations in serious conversation about the one, holy Christian faith is being manifested far and wide.

We cannot ignore the ecumenical movement. We may react to it positively or negatively, we may commend it or condemn it, but we cannot ignore it. Nor should we want to. Lutherans have good reason to be in the forefront of genuine ecumenical endeavor. In their Confessions, the documents that set forth what Lutherans believe, teach, and confess, they are at pains to assert their true catholicity, and they vigorously repudiate sectarianism of all kinds.

Our stance over against other groups professing the Christian faith should be the expression of several basic presuppositions:

1. All Christians are by faith united in one grand fellowship, the body of Christ, the holy Christian church, the communion of saints. This is cause for unending joy and praise. We should thank God for every believer, no matter how frail his faith or how faulty his understanding. The glow of Luther's feeling is unmistakable:

I believe that there is on earth a little holy flock or community of pure saints under one head, Christ. It is called together by the Holy Spirit in one faith, mind, and understanding. It possesses a variety of gifts, yet is united in love without sect or schism. Of this community I also am a part and member, a participant and co-partner in all the blessings it possesses (Large Catechism, Creed, 51-52; Tappert, p. 417).

2. No thoughtful Christian can be indifferent to the many divisions within Christendom or fail to be deeply saddened by the walls that keep individuals and churches apart.

3. Every thoughtful Christian will pray that God would lead all Christians to an ever fuller understanding of His revealed truth, to a stronger faith, a more vigorous hope, a larger love; the ability to recognize, and the courage to overcome error and misunderstanding, and the grace to "speak the truth in love" (Ephesians 4:15), to be concerned about "gaining the brother" (Matthew 18:15), and to "bear one another's burdens" (Galatians 6:2).

Above everything else be sure that you have real deep love for each other, remembering how love can cover a multitude of sins. Serve one another with the particular gifts God has given each of you, as faithful dispensers of the wonderfully varied grace of God. If any of you is a preacher then he should preach his message as from God. And in whatever way a man serves the Chruch he should do it recognising the fact that God gives him his ability, so that God may be glorified in everything through Jesus Christ. To him belong glory and power for ever, amen! (1 Peter 4:8, 10, 11; From J. B. Phillips: *The New Testament in Modern English*, Revised Edition. © J. B. Phillips 1958, 1960, 1972. Used by permission of Macmillan Publishing Co., Inc.)

Bibliography

A. General

Bouman, Walter R. *Christianity American Style*. Dayton, Ohio: Geo. A. Pflaum, Publisher, 1970.

Haselden, Kyle, and Martin E. Marty, eds., *What's Ahead for the Churches? A Report from the Christian Century*. New York: Sheed and Ward, 1964.

Leith, John H. ed. *Creeds of the Churches*. Garden City: Anchor Books. Doubleday & Company, Inc., 1963.

Mayer, F. E. *The Religious Bodies of America*, 4th ed., revised by Arthur Carl Piepkorn. St. Louis: Concordia Publishing House, 1961.

Mead, Frank S. *Handbook of Denominations in the United States*. 5th ed. Nashville: Abingdon Press, 1970.

Neve, J. L. *Churches and Sects of Christendom*. Blair, Nebraska: Lutheran Publishing House, 1952.

Rosten, Leo, ed. *Religions in America*. New York: Simon and Schuster, 1963.

Spitz, Lewis W. Sr. *Our Church and Others*. St. Louis: Concordia Publishing House, 1960.

Spence, Hartzell. *The Story of America's Religions*. New York: Holt, Rinehart and Winston, 1960.

Whalen, William J. *Separated Brethren, A Survey of non-Catholic Christian Denominations*. Milwaukee: The Bruce Publishing Company, 1961.

B. Denominational

Eastern Orthodox

Benz, Ernst. *The Eastern Orthodox Church*. New York: Anchor Books, Doubleday & Company, 1963.

Callinicos, C. N. *The Greek Orthodox Catechism*. New York: Greek Archdiocese of North and South American, 1953.

Mastrantonis, George. *A New-Style Catechism on the Eastern Orthodox Faith for Adults*. St. Louis: The Ologos Mission, 1969.

Ware, Timothy. *The Orthodox Church*. Baltimore: Penguin Books, 1964.

Roman Catholic

Abbott, Walter M., ed. *The Documents of Vatican II*. New York: Guild Press, 1966.

The Church Teaches, Documents of the Church in English Translation. St. Louis: B. Herder Book Co., 1955.

Manz, James G. *Vatican II, Renewal or Reform?* St. Louis: Concordia Publishing House, 1966.

Ott, Ludwig. *The Fundamentals of Catholic Dogma*. St. Louis: B. Herder Book Co., 1954.

Schlink, Edmund. *After the Council*. Philadelphia: Fortress Press, 1968.

Stuber, Stanley I. *Primer on Roman Catholicism for Protestants.* New York: Association Press, 1953.

Lutheran

Tappert, T. G., ed. *The Book of Concord:* The Confessions of the Evangelical Lutheran Church. Philadelphia: Fortress Press, 1959.

Fagerberg, Holsten. *A New Look at the Lutheran Confessions.* St. Louis: Concordia Publishing House, 1972.

Sasse, Herman. *Here We Stand.* New York: Harper & Bros., 1938.

Schlink, Edmund. *Theology of the Lutheran Confessions.* Philadelphia: Fortress Press, 1961.

Episcopalian

The Book of Common Prayer

The Thirty-Nine Articles of Religion, in Leith, *Creeds,* pp. 266 ff.

Neill, Stephen. *Anglicanism.* Baltimore: Penguin Books, 1958.

Calvinistic Reformed

The Book of Confessions, published by The Office of the General Assembly of the United Presbyterian Church in the United States of America.

Calvin, John. *The Institutes of the Christian Religion.* Ed. John T. McNeill, tr. Ford Lewis Battles, in: *The Library of Christian Classics,* Vols. XX and XXI.

Cochrane, Arthur C., ed. *Reformed Confessions of the 16th Century.* Philadelphia: The Westminster Press, 1966.

McNeill, John T. *The History and Character of Calvinism.* New York: Oxford University Press, 1954.

Osterhaven, M. Eugene. *The Spirit of the Reformed Tradition.* Grand Rapids: Wm. B. Eerdmans, 1971.

Torbet, R. G. *A History of the Baptists.* Philadelphia: Judson Press, 1950.

Arminian Reformed

The Articles of Religion, in Leith, *Creeds,* pp. 354 ff.

The Doctrines and Discipline of the Methodist Church. Nashville: The Methodist Publishing House, 1957.

Manual of the History, Doctrine, Government and Ritual of the Church of the Nazarene, 4th ed., Kansas City, Mo: Nazarene Publishing House, c. 1924.

The Constitution of the Pentecostal Fellowship of North America. Springfield, Mo.: Executive Office, General Council, Assemblies of God.

Biederwolf, Wm. E. *Whipping Post Theology.* Grand Rapids: Eerdmans Publ. Co., 1934.

The United Church of Christ

Horton, Douglas. *The United Church of Christ.* New York: Thomas Nelson & Sons, 1962.

The Disciples

Garrison, W. E. *An American Religious Movement.* St. Louis: Bethany Press, 1945.

86

McCormack, *Our Confession of Faith*. Indianapolis: United Christian Missionary Society.

Inner Light Bodies

Anabaptist Confessions, in Leith, *Creeds*, pp. 281 ff.

Mennonite Confession of Faith and Shorter Catechism. Scottdale, Pa.: Herald Press, 1927.

Faith and Practice: Handbook of the Society of Friends. Philadelphia: Friends' Bookstore, 1926

A Brief History of the Amana Society. Amana, Iowa, 1918.

Millennialism

Kromminga, D. H. *The Millennium in the Church*. Grand Rapids: Wm. B. Eerdmans, 1945.

Bass, Clarence B. *Backgrounds to Dispensationalism*. Grand Rapids: Wm. B. Eerdmans, 1960.

Seventh-Day Adventists

Seventh-Day Adventists Answer Questions on Doctrine: An Explanation of Certain Major Aspects of Seventh-Day Adventist Belief. Takoma Park, Washington, D. C.: Review and Herald Publishing Association.

Seboldt, Roland H. A. *What is Seventh-Day Adventism?* St. Louis: Concordia Publishing House, 1959.

The Cults

Gerstner, John H. *The Theology of the Major Sects*. Grand Rapids: Baker Book House, 1960.

Van Baalen, Jan Karel. *The Chaos of Cults*. Grand Rapids: Wm. B. Eerdmans, 2nd ed., 1956.

Jehovah's Witnesses

Martin, Walter R., and Norman H. Klann. *Jehovah of the Watchtower*. Grand Rapids: Zondervan Publishing House, 1953.

Mayer, F. E. *Jehovah's Witnesses*, rev. ed. St. Louis: Concordia Publishing House, 1957.

Schnell, W. J. *Thirty Years a Watchtower Slave*. Grand Rapids: Baker Book House, 1956.

Mormonism

Smith, Joseph. *The Book of Mormon
           The Doctrines and Covenants.
           The Pearl of Great Price.*

Talmage, James E. *Articles of Faith.*

Schumann, F. E. *Is This the Church of Jesus Christ?* St. Louis: Concordia Publishing House, 1943.

Christian Science

Eddy, Mary Baker. *Science and Health with Key to the Scriptures*. Boston: Christian Science Publishing Society.

Dakin, Edward F., *Mrs. Eddy, the Biography of a Virginal Mind*. New York: Charles Scribner's Sons, 1930.

Martin, Walter R., and Norman H. Klann. *The Christian Science Myth*. Paterson, New Jersey: Biblical Truth Publishing Society, Inc., 1954.

Wittmer, George W. *Christian Science in the Light of the Bible*. St. Louis: Concordia Publishing House, 1949.

Study Guide

TO THE DISCUSSION LEADER

This Guide is offered to help you use this book in a class setting. Here you will find discussion questions for each chapter. These questions are designed to form a core of material you can use to think through and discuss the content of the chapters. In every case, the questions are not exhaustive; they are suggestions for the kinds of questions you might want to consider as you work through this material together.

Suggestions for class use of this Guide:

1. You will want to schedule at least 10 sessions in order to deal with each of the sections in this book.

2. You will want to have Bibles, catechisms, and other material (see bibliography) to supplement and inform your discussion. You might research questions which arise in the group yourself, or assign topics to volunteers to report to the class.

3. You will want to read through—and ask the class to read through— the chapter to be discussed before each session. As an alternative you might summarize the material or allow class time for reading, but that will seriously limit your discussion time. A good device for

review is to assign portions of the chapter to volunteers so that they might pay particular attention to those portions in their reading and summarize the content to refresh participants' memories.

4. You will want to select questions you think would be of most value to your group and deal with those first, since you may not be able to cover all of the discussion questions in your allotted time.

5. You will want to encourage open discussion. The purpose of meeting together as a group is to hear as well as speak—to create an atmosphere for people to bring their questions and concerns. Everything you can do to encourage caring and sharing will help make the class more valuable to the participants.

6. You will want to make sure everything is done with attention to the individual. No one should be put on the spot, forced to read or forced to answer. And participants will want to try to be attentive to the need for each person to participate and avoid dominating the discussion.

7. You will want to select a worship leader and, possibly, a class leader for each session.

8. You will want to do all you can to encourage the expression of faith in Jesus Christ and to use the input of the Scriptures to strengthen the relationship in your class and to help the participants grow in their faith life by the power of the Spirit.

Session 1

Chapter 1 THE CHRISTIAN FAITH

1. Have copies of *The Lutheran Hymnal* or other book or booklet with the three ecumenical creeds available for class use.
Divide the group into three smaller groups. Assign each group one of the creeds. Ask them to come up with answers to these two questions:
1) Briefly, what truths are stated in the creed?
2) What is the major emphasis of the creed—the most important truth presented?
It is not necessary that these listings be in great detail and there need not be agreement on the answer to number 2. After 15 minutes, bring the groups together and compare answers.

Beginning on page 7 the author lists those things which Christians have always believed. Read through the following paragraphs as a group and list on the board those things which the author gives as "common" to Christian faith. Compare that list with the lists made from the creeds. Are they the same? Different? How?

From the lists make up a class creed. What form would it take? How would it be like the Apostles' Creed in form and style? What would be emphasized in your creed?

2. In what sense is the church of Christ one? In what sense is it divided? Discuss these questions:

   a. What do you think is the reason for the great diversity of Christian expression?
   b. In what sense is the diversity in the Christian church a good thing?
   c. In what sense is the diversity a dangerous thing and a scandal to others?
   d. What should be the attitude of the Christian toward diversity in the church?
   e. In what sense is our goal the unification of the church of Christ?

3. The author lists the religious freedom in the United States as a reason for the great diversity of Christian expression. What effect do you think some of the following had?
   the move to America to escape religious persecution
   the mixture of nationalities and cultures
   the division between rural and urban people
   poor communication in the early years
   the lack of trained ministers in frontier days
   importation of slaves
   the rise of the women's rights and other rights issues
   exposure to eastern religions
   social unrest caused by depressions, recessions, and the like

4. You are at the airport. You meet a man from India (or some foreign country). His religion is non-Christian and he tells you about his faith.
   You have about 10 minutes before your plane leaves. He asks you: And what is a Christian? How is your religion different from mine?

   What would you say? Work on it individually and then share your responses with the class.

Session 2

Chapter 2 ANCIENT TRADITIONS

1. Note the historical relation of Eastern Orthodoxy to the prevailing social and political powers down through the centuries. How does this compare to the status and liberty granted by the United States government to American Christianity? How do you think the church in America would react if our government tried to exert control or tried to eliminate the church? Would our beliefs or practices change? If so, how?

2. The Orthodox Church holds an optimistic view of man's natural potential. How will this belief influence their other doctrines, especially their teaching concerning man's redemption?

3. Review Rome's concept of "infused grace." According to Roman Catholic teaching what does infused grace enable man to do? Would our Catholic friends maintain that we are saved by faith alone, or by faith *and* good works? Why?

4. Roman Catholics see the celebration of the Mass as a perpetual sacrifice to God for the sins of the living and dead. How does this compare with the Lutheran doctrine of the Lord's Supper? See *Luther's Small Catechism* on Communion and **Hebrews 9:27-28** and **10:11-14** and **Matthew 26:26-29** for help in answering.

5. In conversation, a friend says, "I understand you Lutherans are quite similar to Roman Catholics in teachings and worship." You have about 10 minutes—how would you respond?

Session 3

Chapter 3 EARLY REFORMATION

1. Luther's burning question was, "How may I find a gracious God?" After much prayerful study of Scripture, what answer did he discover? What does that answer mean to you?

2. Lutherans teach that we are justified by grace alone, for Christ's sake alone, through faith alone. Yet we say good works are "necessary." Look at **James 2:14-26.** In what sense are good works necessary?

3. Review the descriptions "high" and "low" church. What can you add? What are the particular advantages and disadvantages of each? Which is most helpful to you?

4. Your neighbor has seen you go to church each Sunday morning and knows that you are very active in your congregation. He finally asks what distinguishes your church from other Christian denominations. In other words, "why are you a Lutheran?" As you formulate your answer, try to think of both the distinctive features of Lutheranism *and* those central truths which you hold in common with all other Christians.

Session 4

Chapter 4 REFORMED CHURCHES OF THE CALVINIST TRADITION

1. Based on his notion of the absolute sovereignty of God, John Calvin taught "double predestination," that is, some are elected to salvation, others to damnation. What effect will such a doctrine have on an individual as he or she strives to lead the Christian life? What is the danger involved if the person is arrogantly convinced she is one of the elect? What if one fears he is "chosen" to be damned?

2. In the Calvinist Reformed tradition, who is "active" in the sacraments, God or man? Who is "active" according to the Lutheran understanding (see the *Small Catechism*)? How does the Calvinists' emphasis influence their understanding of Baptism and the Lord's Supper?

3. Note the differences between Calvinism and Arminianism (see the Table on page   ). Of the combined list of ten points, Lutherans agree with two of them. Which are they? Go through the two lists and explain why we agree or disagree with each of the points.

4. The Baptist church exhibits a wide range of theological and doctrinal variety among its many different branches. What features of their system of church government would lend to such variety?

5. *For Further Study.* Assign someone to do a comparison of the teachings of Luther, Zwingli, and Calvin. Use the material in this book and other available resources. A report to the class and discussion might follow.

Session 5

Chapter 5 REFORMED CHURCHES OF THE ARMINIAN TRADITION

1. The Wesley brothers were troubled by the injustice, inequality, and empty formalism they saw in their Anglican church. As a result, their religious emphasis was on faith-life rather than doctrine. Why was their emphasis valid for their time? How did it help? Is the same emphasis necessary in the church today? Why? How would you go about changing similar problems in the church today?

2. Evaluate the claim of the Holiness bodies that "born again" Christians are transformed instantly into a state in which they no longer commit willful sins and are thereby entirely sanctified. Compare this teaching to the Lutheran emphasis on our state as sinner and saint. Which point of view seems more valid as you watch people? Why?

3. Evaluate the claim that the initial evidence of the baptism in the Holy Spirit is "speaking in tongues." What are some of the dangers of such a claim? What are the implications of the teaching that "real" Christians experience two "baptisms"? See the *Small Catechism* for assistance.

Session 6

Chapter 6 ATTEMPTS AT OVERCOMING DENOMINATIONALISM

1. Review the three ways of dealing with the problem of denominationalism. Do you think it is possible to "recognize the differences among churches but regard them as nondivisive and establish a common doctrinal denominator"? Why or why not?

2. Do you believe it is possible to discard the historical denominations and recapture the church of the New Testament era? Why or why not? What about attempts to discard all labels and theological terms not found in the New Testament, virtually eliminating creeds and confessions? Possible? Why or why not?

3. Some people have held that the church must either "merge, or be submerged"; their rationale being that in the face of the secular-

ization of our culture we must present a united front against the enemies of the church. How would you respond?

4. Your neighbor—a very religious person—says, "What is important is how we live as Christians, not what we believe." How would you respond?

Session 7

Chapter 7 THE INNER LIGHT

1. For the Mennonites the Gospel is called "the law of Christ in which the whole counsel and will of God are comprehended," and salvation is linked to the personal piety of the member through his mystical union with Christ. What do such notions presuppose about the capabilities of man? How do they relate to the doctrine of salvation by grace alone for Christ's sake?

2. How is the Quaker teaching of the "Inward Light" similar to or different from the doctrine of man's creation in the image of God?

3. How does the Quakers' teaching of the inborn goodness of man relate to their claim that no means are required to bring God in from without, hence no clergy, preaching, sacraments, or churches. What would you define as the way of salvation according to the Quakers?

4. Nearly all of these groups arose as a protest against the laxity they saw in their own denominations. How would you react if you perceived a similar situation today? What would you tell a friend who wanted to start his own more disciplined, pious group in opposition to the casual ways of the established church body?

Session 8

Chapter 8 THE MILLENNIUM

1. Historically, hopes for the early return of Christ have flourished at times of great social distress or religious persecution. Why? How about today—is the topic of the millennium current? Why or why not?

2. A friend says, "I know the exact date of Christ's return. I have calculated it from the numbers in **Daniel** and **Revelation**." How would you respond?

3. Relate the principles of millennialism to some of the speculation concerning the nature and destiny of Israel and the Jewish people. Read **Romans 9—11** in this connection. How do you interpret the Pauline assertion that "all Israel will be saved" (**Romans 11:26**)? The context will help you arrive at a Biblical answer.

4. Cite some of the implications the millennial teaching has for the preaching of the Gospel *today*. Will our preaching be more or less urgent? Why? In what sense is the claim that the second coming of Christ is an important emphasis valid?

Session 9

Chapter 9 THE CULTS

1. What position is generally given to Jesus Christ by the cults described in this chapter? How is that position different from that given by your church?

2. Compare the teachings of the three main cults. In each case, what is the source of religious knowledge? How do those claims fit with our emphasis on Scripture as "the only source and norm" for teaching?

3. Is there any "good news" (gospel) in the Jehovah's Witnesses' teachings? If so, what is it? If not, what seems to be the central thrust of their teaching?

4. What is the particular appeal of Mormonism for many people? Why are Christians in an even better position to stress these praiseworthy characteristics than Mormons?

5. What happens to the Christian doctrine of the forgiveness of sins for Christ's sake in the Christian Scientist's philosophical system? Why?

6. Mature Christians need to be able to evaluate the claims of any system of truth that offers itself for consideration and acceptance. How can we best avoid the deception involved in the cults? How can

we help others from being taken in by them? In dealing with people involved in the cults, what would you say to them and what points would you stress?

Session 10

Chapter 10 CONCLUDING REFLECTIONS

1. The author poses crucial questions in discussing the abundance of denominations: *Are there* legitimate spiritual needs that we have failed to meet? *Are there* accents in our theology that have been forgotten? If so, what are they? If not, how do you account for the spiritual turmoil in our church?

2. Evaluate John Wesley's observation that Luther wrote well on redemption through Christ (justification), but misunderstood the cause of and way of Christian living (sanctification). How do you understand the relationship between justification and sanctification?

3. Do you agree with the assertion that the absence of real concern for social issues among Lutherans is due to their primary emphasis on God's grace, thus devaluating man's activity? If that is true, what can be done to correct the imbalance? If not, to what do you attribute the relative lack of social activity among Lutherans?

4. What is the ultimate purpose of all Holy Scripture? (See **John 20:31**). How does the knowledge of this overriding purpose help us both in our own study and in our evaluation of the teachings of other religious groups?

5. Review the basic presuppositions affecting our relationship to other Christian groups. What value are they to you? See if you can come up with a statement of purpose which would take seriously our need to demonstrate Christian love while not diminishing Biblical truth.

    Start: In dealing with other Christians we should. . . .